1987

GEN
LOCKE
CL

W9-BAV-573

3 0301 00053035 8

CLASSICS IN EDUCATION
Lawrence A. Cremin, General Editor

☆ ☆ ☆

THE REPUBLIC AND THE SCHOOL
Horace Mann on the Education of Free Men
Edited by Lawrence A. Cremin

AMERICAN IDEAS ABOUT ADULT EDUCATION
1710–1951
Edited by C. Hartley Grattan

DEWEY ON EDUCATION
Introduction and Notes by Martin S. Dworkin

THE SUPREME COURT AND EDUCATION
Edited by David Fellman

INTERNATIONAL EDUCATION
A Documentary History
Edited by David G. Scanlon

CRUSADE AGAINST IGNORANCE
Thomas Jefferson on Education
Edited by Gordon C. Lee

CHINESE EDUCATION UNDER COMMUNISM
Edited by Chang-tu Hu

CHARLES W. ELIOT AND POPULAR EDUCATION
Edited by Edward A. Krug

WILLIAM T. HARRIS ON EDUCATION
(in preparation)
Edited by Martin S. Dworkin

THE *EMILE* OF JEAN JACQUES ROUSSEAU
Selections
Translated and Edited by William Boyd

THE MINOR EDUCATIONAL WRITINGS OF
JEAN JACQUES ROUSSEAU
Selected and Translated by William Boyd

PSYCHOLOGY AND THE SCIENCE OF EDUCATION
Selected Writings of Edward L. Thorndike
Edited by Geraldine M. Joncich

THE NEW-ENGLAND PRIMER
Introduction by Paul Leicester Ford

BENJAMIN FRANKLIN ON EDUCATION
Edited by John Hardin Best

THE COLLEGES AND THE PUBLIC
1787–1862
Edited by Theodore Rawson Crane

TRADITIONS OF AFRICAN EDUCATION
Edited by David G. Scanlon

NOAH WEBSTER'S AMERICAN SPELLING BOOK
Introductory Essay by Henry Steele Commager

EMERSON ON EDUCATION
Selections
Edited by Howard Mumford Jones

ECONOMIC INFLUENCES UPON EDUCATIONAL
PROGRESS IN THE UNITED STATES, 1820–1850
By Frank Tracy Carlton
Foreword by Lawrence A. Cremin

QUINTILIAN ON EDUCATION
Selected and Translated by William M. Smail

ROMAN EDUCATION FROM CICERO
TO QUINTILIAN
By Aubrey Gwynn, S.J.

HERBERT SPENCER ON EDUCATION
Edited by Andreas M. Kazamias

JOHN LOCKE'S *OF THE CONDUCT
OF THE UNDERSTANDING*
Edited by Francis W. Garforth

John Locke's
Of the Conduct
of the Understanding

Edited, with an Introduction and Notes, by
FRANCIS W. GARFORTH

CLASSICS IN

No. 31

EDUCATION

TEACHERS COLLEGE PRESS
TEACHERS COLLEGE, COLUMBIA UNIVERSITY
NEW YORK

Foreword

Locke's treatise *Of the Conduct of the Understanding*
differs significantly in style and format from its prede-
cessor, *Some Thoughts Concerning Education*. The
Thoughts took form in a series of letters to Edward
Clarke on the rearing of his children, and the work itself
bears the characteristic marks of its origin: it is loosely
drawn, often repetitive, and generally informal in tone.
The *Conduct*, on the other hand, was initially conceived
as an addendum to the *Essay Concerning Human Understanding*, and is in the character of that *Essay*, although
at the same time more systematic and more abstruse. It
can be read, as Mr. Garforth points out, both as an
extension of the *Essay*, indicating the practical implications of the doctrines set forth there, and as a complement to the *Thoughts*, elaborating in particular those
principles that apply to the cultivation of the intellect.

Yet the cast of the *Thoughts* and the *Conduct* is essen-
tially the same. Taken together, they stand squarely
within the tradition of Elyot's *Governour*, Brathwait's
English Gentleman, and Chesterfield's *Letters*, as courtesy
books addressed to the problem of educating a ruling
class. They assume, in the fashion of the genre, that the
ideal training for leadership takes place, not in schools
and universities, but within the family, and they sketch
the principles for making that training noble, responsi-
ble, and effective.

Twentieth-century Americans, instructed by the his-
tories of Paul Monroe, Frank P. Graves, and others, have
tended to view Locke as a "formalist" in education, cit-

ing as evidence his assertions in the *Conduct* regarding the role of particular studies in the training of the mind. But such a reading is oversimplified—as Stephen Duggan and V. T. Thayer pointed out years ago—as well as anachronistic, for as it construes a seventeenth-century pedagogical treatise in the terms of nineteenth-century theories of formal discipline. Locke was far too wise a man to argue either that the intellect can be disciplined by concentration on a few well-chosen studies or that there is so little transfer of training as to make all talk of intellectual discipline senseless. He merely assumed, as present-day educators are coming again to recognize, that one crucial element of any education is learning how to learn, and that some approaches to this task are perhaps more valuable than others. It is Locke's formulation of the problem as well as the particular solutions he proposed that make the *Conduct* contemporary and worthy of the most careful study and consideration.

LAWRENCE A. CREMIN

Contents

☆   ☆   ☆

Introduction

By FRANCIS W. GARFORTH

It is impossible in this brief introduction to give a detailed account of Locke's full and varied life. Those who want such an account must turn to the biographies of Fox Bourne and Cranston or to the brief summaries in the editions of *Some Thoughts Concerning Education* mentioned in the bibliography. However, some knowledge of Locke's main interests and activities is essential to understanding *Of the Conduct of the Understanding*.

Locke went to Christ Church, Oxford, in 1652, where he received the bachelor's degree in 1656 and the master's two years later. The way seemed open for an academic career, and he was in fact elected to a lectureship in Greek in 1660; but in the meantime other interests had claimed his attention. In the seventeenth century a great part of the student's training consisted of exercises in formal logic and disputation which were an inheritance from the scholastic disciplines of the Middle Ages. Locke was sickened by these, for they seemed to him futile and irrelevant, neither training the mind nor leading it in the path of knowledge (see, for instance, *Essay Concerning Human Understanding* IV, xvii and *Of the Conduct of the Understanding*, sections 7, 29, 31 etc.) Partly for this reason, and partly, no doubt, because of temperament and character, he was attracted to a very different approach to knowledge and learning which was then being developed by a group of men at Oxford. Chief of these was Robert Boyle, best known now for his "law" on the volume and pressure of gases.

The aim of these men was not to seek knowledge by arguing deductively from a priori principles to supposed fact, which was the method of the scholastic logic derived from Aristotle; instead they sought by patient observation and experiment to arrive at a knowledge based on evidence, a knowledge which represented the world as it actually is, not as it is portrayed (often falsely) by human presupposition. They were laying the foundations of modern scientific method, which, though it employs deductive logic in exploring the consequences of its hypotheses, is founded on observation and the conclusions inferred inductively from it. The activities and discussions of these men led to the foundation of the Royal Society, of which Locke himself became a Fellow some years later. He associated himself with them, became a friend of Boyle (who was five years older), and assisted him in some of his experiments. No doubt it was at a meeting with some of them that there was sown the seed which grew into his major philosophical work, the *Essay Concerning Human Understanding;* Locke describes it thus in the Epistle to the Reader which prefaces the book:

Were it fit to trouble thee with the history of this *Essay,* I should tell thee that five or six friends, meeting at my chamber and discoursing on a subject very remote from this, found themselves quickly at a stand by the difficulties that rose on every side. After we had awhile puzzled ourselves, without coming any nearer a resolution of those doubts which perplexed us, it came into my thoughts that we took a wrong course; and that before we set ourselves upon enquiries of that nature, it was necessary to examine our own abilities, and see what objects our understandings were, or were not, fitted to deal with.

Within his wider interest in science Locke had developed a particular attachment to medicine and had devoted considerable time to its study. In 1666 he applied for the degree of Doctor of Medicine; the application was unsuccessful, but he was eventually, in 1674, awarded both the bachelor's degree and a faculty to practise. His medical studies led to another important friendship, with the eminent physician Thomas Sydenham, whose experimental approach to medicine was entirely in accord with his own outlook. Thus Locke's interest in science was far from merely theoretical; in the practice of medicine he had the opportunity to apply and to elaborate the principles and methods he had learnt from Boyle and his Oxford associates.

Locke developed another major interest during his years at Oxford, namely in politics and civil affairs. This, like his interest in science, remained with him for the rest of his life and indeed came to occupy more of his time than any other. In 1665 he was appointed secretary to a brief diplomatic mission; shortly after his return he was introduced to Lord Ashley (later the Earl of Shaftesbury) and was appointed his personal physician. In fact his responsibilities were far wider than this; he also acted as Ashley's secretary and adviser and as tutor to his son and grandson. Through Lord Ashley, Locke became involved in the political intrigues of his time, which resulted eventually in the revolution of 1688, the overthrow of James II, and the accession of William. For a time it seems that he may have been in danger of his life; at any rate he fled to Holland and remained there for six years in a kind of voluntary exile. From his return in 1689 almost to the end of his life in 1704 he held various official posts which kept him in close touch with the government; such, for instance, was his membership of the Council of Trade.

It can be seen from this sketch of Locke's interests and activities that he was no cloistered academic but a man of wide and varied experience who wrote, not as a spectator, but as one deeply involved in the political and intellectual movements of his time. The range of his experience is reflected in his writings. Of these the most important is his *Essay Concerning Human Understanding,* which was begun about 1670, finished during his sojourn in Holland, and finally published in 1690. More will be said of this later. His political works include the *Epistola de Tolerantia* (1689), a *Second* and *Third Letter Concerning Toleration* (1690 and 1692), *Two Treatises of Government* (1689), and various papers on financial policy. He also wrote *The Reasonableness of Christianity* (1695) and various notes and an essay (these posthumously published) on the letters of St. Paul. His educational writings include *Some Thoughts Concerning Education,* about which more will be said later, and (if one chooses so to regard it) *Of the Conduct of the Understanding.* Locke's qualifications for writing on education were by no means as strong as those in philosophy and politics, but apart from his tutorships within the Ashley family he had also taken charge for two years of the son of a wealthy merchant, Sir John Banks, during a period of residence in France. Moreover, it is obvious from what he writes that he had had close contact with children (he was never married himself) and opportunity for observing them.

Of the Conduct of the Understanding was intended by Locke to be an additional chapter to his *Essay Concerning Human Understanding.* He writes of his intention in a letter to William Molyneux, dated April 10, 1697:

I have lately got a little leisure to think of some additions to my book, against the next edition, and within these few days have fallen upon a subject that I know not how far it will lead me. I have writ several pages on it, but the matter, the further I go, opens the more upon me, and I cannot yet get any sight of the end of it. The title of the chapter will be "Of the Conduct of the Understanding," which if I pursue as far as I imagine it will reach, and as it deserves, will, I conclude, make the largest chapter in my *Essay*.

However, *Conduct* did not appear in the next edition of the *Essay;* it was published posthumously and without final revision in 1706, together with other hitherto unpublished writings (see the "Advertisement to the Reader," which precedes the text of *Conduct*). The work is thus related in its conception to the *Essay*, but in its content, though the kinship with the *Essay* is obvious, it is more closely linked with *Some Thoughts Concerning Education*. It can be read either as an extension of the *Essay*, indicating the practical implications of the doctrines there set forth, or it can be read as an addition to Locke's educational writings, extending and in some measure complementing the account of education given in *Thoughts*. It can also be read for itself, as a practical manual on "clear thinking," a statement of the pitfalls that lie in the road to truth and the means by which the mind can be trained to avoid them. Before proceeding to an examination of the content of *Conduct*, we shall first look at some of the leading doctrines of these two other works.

The *Essay* is a very big book, both in the obvious sense (for it runs to over four hundred pages even in the abridged edition of Professor Woozley) and in its impact on British philosophy. In it Locke asked and attempted to answer certain fundamental questions about the sources and nature of knowledge and about the powers and limitations of the human mind. He was not the first, of course, to raise epistemological problems, for philosophers had been doing this from before the time of Plato; but he was the first, in Professor O'Connor's words, "to insist that the nature and capacities of the human mind should be the starting-point for philosophy."[1] The origin of the work in the meeting with his friends is described in the quotation above; its purpose, Locke states, is

to enquire into the original, certainty and extent of human knowledge, together with the grounds and degrees of belief, opinion and assent.[2]

The central thesis of the *Essay* is that all our knowledge derives ultimately from experience. At birth the mind is like an empty cabinet or a blank sheet of paper, "void of all characters, without any ideas";[3] it has no innate ideas or principles "which the soul receives in its very first being and brings into the world with it."[4] Whence, then, Locke asks, does it acquire

that vast store which the busy and boundless fancy of man has painted on it with an almost endless variety? Whence has it all the materials of reason and knowledge?[5]

He continues:

To this I answer, in one word, from EXPERIENCE; in that all our knowledge is founded and from that it ultimately derives itself.[6]

This is not to deny that the mind has innate potentialities or that heredity is a determining factor in human attainment—"Amongst men of equal education there is

---

[1] D. J. O'Connor, *John Locke* (Harmondsworth, England: Penguin Books, 1952), p. 222.
[2] *An Essay Concerning Human Understanding* (cited hereafter as *Essay*), I, i, 2.
[3] *Ibid.*, I, ii, 15; II, i, 2.
[4] *Ibid.*, I, ii, 1.
[5] *Ibid.*, II, i, 2.
[6] *Ibid.*

great inequality of parts," he tells us in *Conduct*.[7] Locke was too keen an observer to overlook the obvious fact of the inequality of human endowment. What he does deny is that the mind brings with it into the world any epistemological *content,* or that knowledge is a reminiscence, as Plato suggested, of something learnt in a previous existence.

What, then, are the materials of knowledge? We are all aware, Locke says, that we think, and that what the "mind is applied about whilst thinking" is "the ideas that are there."[8] "Ideas" come from two sources within experience, namely, sensation and reflection:

Our observation employed either about external sensible objects, or about the internal operations of our minds perceived and reflected on by ourselves, is that which supplies our understandings with all the materials of thinking. These two are the fountains of knowledge, from whence all the ideas we have, or can naturally have, do spring. First, our senses, conversant about particular sensible objects, do convey into the mind several distinct perceptions of things, according to those various ways wherein those objects do affect them. And thus we come by those *ideas* we have of *yellow, white, heat, cold, soft, hard, bitter, sweet,* and all those which we call sensible qualities. . . . Secondly, the other fountain from which experience furnisheth the understanding with ideas is the perception of the operations of our own mind within us, as it is employed about the ideas it has got. . . . And such are *perception, thinking, doubting, believing, reasoning, knowing, willing,* and all the different actings of our own minds.[9]

From these two sources comes "our whole stock of ideas; . . . we have nothing in our minds which did not

[7] *Of the Conduct of the Understanding* (cited hereafter as *Conduct*), section 2; cf. *Some Thoughts Concerning Education* (cited hereafter as *Thoughts*), §§ 1, 101

[8] *Essay,* II, i, 1.

[9] *Ibid.,* II, i, 2–4.

come in one of these two ways."[10] "Ideas" are either
simple or complex. Simple "ideas" are *given;* that is to
say, they are offered to us ready-made, and so long as
sense and thought are active we can neither reject nor
alter them; they are the basic raw material of knowledge
and must be accepted as they are. Yet, although in the
initial receiving of them the mind is passive, it has the
power to combine them to form complex "ideas"; this
it does, thereby adding to the range and content of its
own reflection. (It can also *relate* "ideas," both simple
and complex, and *abstract* them to form general truths.)
Locke says a great deal more about "ideas"—they are the
subject of Book II of the *Essay*—but the brief account
given here is sufficient for the understanding of *Conduct.*

In Book IV (after an extremely interesting discussion
of language in Book III) Locke proceeds to examine
the nature of knowledge:

Since the mind, in all its thoughts and reasonings, hath no
other immediate object but its own ideas . . . it is evident that
our knowledge is only conversant about them.[11]

In what, then, does it consist? It is, he says, "the perception of the connexion and agreement or disagreement and repugnancy of any of our ideas."[12] When we
have the assurance that certain "ideas" "agree" or "disagree," then we have knowledge. He instances the perception that white is not black and that the sum of the
internal angles of a triangle is equal to that of two right
angles. He elaborates this by indicating four kinds of
agreement and disagreement, but it is unnecessary to follow him into the details of his explanation. More important is his division of knowledge into three kinds or, as

10 *Ibid.,* 5.
11 *Ibid.,* IV, i, 1.
12 *Ibid.,* 2.

he calls them, "degrees"; these are intuitive, demonstrative, and "sensitive."

Intuitive knowledge is apprehended immediately without any process of reasoning:

In this the mind is at no pains of proving or examining, but perceives the truth as the eye doth light, only by being directed towards it. Thus the mind perceives that white is not black, that a circle is not a triangle. . . .[13]

Demonstrative knowledge, which Locke for various reasons regards as inferior to intuitive, is reached by inference through one or more "intermediate ideas" from premiss to conclusion; an obvious example is the deductive reasoning of mathematics. Both of these degrees of knowledge offer certainty; one can be sure of their validity. The third and lowest degree is what Locke calls "sensitive" knowledge, by which he means an apprehension of the objects of the external world by means of our senses. This is not properly knowledge (by Locke's definition), since it does not offer certainty, but

going beyond bare probability, and yet not reaching perfectly to either of the foregoing degrees of certainty, passes under the name of knowledge.[14]

In demonstrative knowledge a single train of valid reasoning is sufficient to provide certainty in the conclusion; sensitive knowledge, however, requires numerous trains to establish the conclusion with sufficient probability to command assent. Locke is here pointing to the distinction between deductive reasoning, whose conclusions are certainly true if the inference is valid, and inductive reasoning, whose conclusions can never be more than probable. He is also pointing to the importance of

[13] *Ibid.,* ii, 1.
[14] *Ibid.,* 14.

probability as a criterion of knowledge and to its place in the procedures of science.

It is not difficult to find weaknesses in Locke's epistemology. Despite his claim to establish knowledge exclusively on experience, there remain in his thought strong traces of the traditional rationalism which still dominated the schools and universities. Such, for instance, are his demand that knowledge must be certain and his use of terms like "substance" and "essence" which were part of the stock-in-trade of scholastic thought but had little to contribute to the new empiricism. Yet Locke should not be too severely criticised; no innovator can extricate himself completely from the modes of thought he is trying to displace; and Locke deserves the fullest credit for his reorientation of epistemological enquiry. It may also be objected that Locke confused philosophy and psychology, that he attempted by reason alone to answer questions about the operation of the mind which only the fullest and most patient investigation was capable of resolving, and that he was thus untrue to his professed empiricism. But in the seventeenth century philosophy and psychology were not yet differentiated (nor were they for another two hundred years), and the idea that the mind itself can be subjected, like other natural phenomena, to observation and experiment was still in the process of gestation. It can be further argued that, partly as a result of this, Locke's account of mind is too mechanical—as though it were indeed an "empty cabinet" to be stored with contents or a "blank sheet" waiting for the pen, instead of (in the more appropriate imagery of William James) a "stream of consciousness." The criticism is just but should not be overpressed; no man can think two centuries ahead of his time or anticipate conclusions which are the fruit of long processes of investigation and intellectual growth.

Perhaps the most serious charge, however, is that of unclarity in the use of his central concept, "idea." Sense perception, we are told, gives us "ideas," and so does reflection; but "yellow," "white," "heat," etc. are totally unlike "perception," "thinking," etc., and to call them by the same name is at best confusing, at worst incompetent. Indeed the range of "ideas" is so wide—"space," "motion," "solidity," "pain," "existence," "unity," etc. —that their inclusion within a single category under the name of "idea" is evidently hazardous unless preceded by a careful analysis of each "idea"—and after this it might well seem impossible. Nor is it by any means obvious that the "ideas" which he instances as "simple" are possessed of that "uncompounded . . . uniform appearance"[15] which he attributes to them. Certainly Locke should have given more thought to his "ideas"; the brief account in Book I is altogether too hasty and facile.[16] Moreover, by leaving so much unclear he opens the way to further criticism; for if "ideas" of sensation are representations of an original sense impression, and if the mind knows only its own "ideas," not the originals which they represent, how can we be sure either that there is a world external to us or that "ideas" faithfully represent it?[17] It can be said in mitigation, however, that

[15] *Ibid.*, II, ii, 1.

[16] "It being that term which, I think, serves best to stand for whatsoever is the *object* of the understanding when a man thinks, I have used it to express whatever is meant by *phantasm, notion, species,* or *whatever it is which the mind can be employed about in thinking*" (*Essay,* I, i, 8). For further discussion of Locke's "ideas," see Professor Woozley's introduction to his edition, *John Locke: An Essay Concerning Human Understanding,* abridged (London: William Collins Sons & Co., 1964), pp. 24 ff.

[17] Locke anticipates the first part of this criticism in *Essay,* IV,

as Locke was blazing a trail, it was impossible for him to smooth out every tangle in his path, and that, since his aim was to present in general terms an empirical account of knowledge, he was more concerned, as Professor Woozley says,[18] to use the notion of "idea" than to talk about it.

We turn now to *Some Thoughts Concerning Education*. While Locke was in Holland, he was asked by a Mr. Edward Clarke, a gentleman friend who lived in Somerset, for advice on the upbringing of his son, then a child of eight. The letters which Locke wrote back from time to time constituted the first draft of the book, which was published in 1693 and considerably enlarged in later editions. In its immediate purpose, therefore, the book is restricted to the education of upper-class boys, but in effect a great deal of it is of quite general application. *Thoughts* is, in fact, one of the wisest books on education ever written, anticipating again and again the best of modern educational thought and practice. The purpose of the book does, however, impose on Locke the expression of a view of academic learning which is liable to misinterpretation:

Reading and writing and learning I allow to be necessary, but yet not the chief business. . . . Learning must be had, but in the second place, as subservient only to greater qualities.[19]

All that he is saying is that in a gentleman, character, good breeding, and the successful management of his affairs are more important than scholarship—a sentiment with which few would disagree. Taken with numerous

---

iv, 3: "How shall the mind, when it perceives nothing but its own ideas, know that they agree with things themselves?"

[18] Woozley, *op. cit.*, p. 30.

[19] *Thoughts*, § 147.

similar statements, this may lead the reader to suppose that Locke was prejudiced against books and learning generally; and this is not the case. It is for this reason that *Conduct* is a valuable complement to *Thoughts* balancing the view there expressed with a forthright demand for a vigorous training of the intellect.

Despite their difference in purpose, there is a broad similarity of approach between the two books, as well as agreement in numerous points of detail. The most obvious example is the empiricism which underlies them both; in *Conduct* the expression of this is closer to the *Essay*, whose contents and terminology it constantly echoes; in *Thoughts* it appears more often, but no less persistently in educational terms. "Truth," we read in *Thoughts*, "is to be found and supported by a mature and due consideration of things themselves";[20] and it is in "things that fall under the senses" that "our knowledge should begin and in those things be laid the foundation."[21] It can be seen also in Locke's insistence on the need to observe children in order that their abilities may be known and teaching methods may be accommodated to them;[22] in his emphasis on practice and habit as instruments of learning in preference to precept and wholesale memorisation;[23] and in his remarks on the origin of fear in children.[24]

There are many other similarities between the two books. In both Locke appeals to the criterion of utility: the value of truths "is to be measured by their usefulness and tendency," he tells us in *Conduct*;[25] and in *Thoughts:*

[20] *Ibid.*, § 189.
[21] *Ibid.*, § 166.
[22] See, for example, *ibid.*, §§ 66, 101–102.
[23] See, for example, *ibid.*, §§ 64–65, 98.
[24] *Ibid.*, § 138.
[25] *Conduct*, section 25.

Most time and application is to be bestowed on that which is
like to be of greatest consequence and frequentest use in the
ordinary course and occurrences of that life the young man is
designed for.[26]

In both, while granting the fact of native endowment,
he insists on the power of education and training to
raise the level of attainment:

Of all the men we meet with nine parts of ten are what they
are, good or evil, useful or not, by their education. 'Tis that
which makes the great difference in mankind.[27]

And in *Conduct:*

We are born with faculties and powers capable almost of
anything . . . but it is only the exercise of those powers which
gives us ability and skill in anything and leads us towards
perfection.[28]

We find, too, the same liberal view of education as
aimed not so much at specific knowledge as at imbuing
children with the skills and habits which will enable
them to explore unaided any field of enquiry that at-
tracts them. For instance, compare pages 63 and 71-72
with the following from *Thoughts:*

[In that] which concerns a young gentleman's studies his tutor
should remember that his business is not so much to teach him
all that is knowable as to raise in him a love and esteem of
knowledge and to put him in the right way of knowing and
improving himself when he has a mind to it.[29]

There is much else that *Thoughts* and *Conduct* have in
common—Locke's firm good sense, his understanding of
young people,[30] his robust and manly attitude to life, his

[26] *Thoughts,* § 198.
[27] *Ibid.,* § 1.
[28] *Conduct,* section 4.
[29] *Thoughts,* § 195.
[30] For his sympathy with and understanding of young people, see
Conduct, section 30 and also *Thoughts,* §§ 63, 71, 145.

intellectual integrity; but it would be tedious to add further examples. The student of *Conduct* can get by without reading the *Essay* (though he would lose by the omission); but *Thoughts* is a classic of both education and literature, and to read it is both a duty and a delight.

It is the purpose of this edition to encourage students to read *Conduct* for themselves. It may be helpful, however, to indicate some of its major themes and to add some general observations about it. Its basic empiricism has already been pointed out; Locke's viewpoint is dominated by the epistemological assumptions of the *Essay*. "We are born ignorant of everything," he says; the structure of knowledge comes of our own building as we train ourselves to observe and reflect on the world around us and to use critically the observations of others. As far as possible knowledge should be firsthand:

Knowing is seeing, and, if it be so, it is madness to persuade ourselves that we do so by another man's eyes. . . . Till we ourselves see it with our own eyes and perceive it by our own understandings, we are as much in the dark and as void of knowledge as before, let us believe any learned author as much as we will.

Facts and things as they present themselves to our observation are the test of truth, not preconceived notions accepted secondhand from others or suggested by our own prejudices. Coupled with this is Locke's aversion from the scholastic logic and from the minute and irrelevant disputations which were its practical manifestation in education. He attacks its specious terminology, its false picture of knowledge, the narrowness and superficiality of its arguments. He speaks slightingly of "logical chicaners" compared with the "man of reason," and distinguishes those who are serious in the pursuit of learn-

ing from those who "deceive and swell themselves with a
a little articulated air." The scholastic methods were so
incompatible with his empiricism, so alien to his whole
approach to knowledge (indeed to life), that criticism
of them overflows from his pen as a by-product of the
presentation of his own case.

The subject of the book is the training of the mind so
that it may more readily attain to the truth. Locke's
approach is both negative and positive, warning against
the obstacles to intellectual fitness as well as suggesting
methods of securing it. He cautions against lack of con-
ceptual clarity, against the indiscriminate use of analogy, against prejudice and hasty judgement, against one-
sidedness in argument and the facile acceptance of views
which are merely popular or hallowed by antiquity. On
the positive side he points to the importance of practice
in establishing mental discipline, of carefully examining
the premises of argument, of impartiality in judgement
and of the need to seek evidence and to obey it. Especially interesting, both for its sound advice and its insight into human weakness is his discussion of prejudice.
He is aware of its many sources—in party allegiance,
emotional bias, conservatism, antipathy to the new,
blindness to one's own deficiencies, and even sheer laziness ("few men care to be instructed but at an easy
rate"). He knows how easy is self-deception, how firmly
we adhere to our earliest conclusions, how reluctant we
are to accept the discipline of careful investigation, how
readily content with a partial or superficial view.

There is much other excellent advice in *Conduct,*
both general and particular. Locke urges his readers to
persevere in the pursuit of knowledge, neither under-
estimating the difficulties nor underrating their own
powers:

Nature commonly lodges her treasure and jewels in rocky ground. If the matter be knotty and the sense lies deep, the mind must stop and buckle to it and stick upon it with labour and thought and close contemplation, and not leave it till it has mastered the difficulty and got possession of truth.

And to the diffident he says (quoting a proverb): " 'Use legs and have legs.' Nobody knows what strength of parts he has till he has tried them." More can be done by steady application and practice than seems possible:

When the mind by insensible degrees has brought itself to attention and close thinking, it will be able to cope with difficulties and master them without any prejudice to itself, and then it may go on roundly.

Time is short and must be used with due care and economy: "Nobody is under an obligation to know everything," but even the one day's rest in seven, "had they no other idle hours," would enable men to advance in knowledge,

if they would but make use of these vacancies from their daily labour and apply themselves to an improvement of knowledge with as much diligence as they often do to a great many other things that are useless.

Especially noteworthy are Locke's comments on the proper use of books. He distinguishes reading from understanding, the mere passage through a printed text from the careful examination of its content:

We are of the ruminating kind and it is not enough to cram ourselves with a great load of collections; unless we chew them over again, they will not give us strength and nourishment.

Notable too are his observations on procedure in the solution of intellectual problems: it is essential to "state the question right and see whereon it turns." Then:

In every question the nature and manner of the proof it is
capable of should first be considered to make our enquiry such
as it should be.

Moreover, it should not be assumed that a method
found suitable in one field of knowledge can be usefully
applied to another, where, in fact, "it serves only to
perplex and confound the understanding." Here Locke
is thoroughly modern; so he is too in his comments on
language. This subject occupies the whole of *Essay*
Book III (note especially Chapters ix through xi), and
he has no need to repeat himself in *Conduct;* but he re-
minds his readers that the basic function of language is
to communicate, that the meaning of words is in their
use, not in themselves, and that, however well established in academic tradition, they are nevertheless
"empty sounds without a meaning" unless they correspond to some clearly conceived idea in the mind.

Its other qualities apart, *Conduct* is valuable for the
whole outlook on life and learning that it embodies.
Here we find a healthy scorn of narrowmindedness and
bigotry, of intellectual sloth and sham; we find a persis-
tent encouragement to initiative and effort in the pursuit of knowledge, a refusal to accept as final the limitations of natural endowment. Here there is confidence in
human reason and an optimistic assessment of the power
of truth—"truth is always the same; time alters it not";
its claim is stronger than that of personal interest, and
factual evidence is its sufficient support. The character
of Locke himself shines through the book—his patent
integrity of character and motive, the subordination of
self to fact and principle, the courteous good humour,
the wisdom born of a life of varied service to the causes
to which he felt committed. To read it carefully and
reflectively—ruminating, as Locke himself recommends

—is an experience of great educational value: it serves as a mirror to oneself in its disclosure of intellectual impediment; it is a guide to mental discipline and clarity of thought; at the same time it invigorates by its contact with the man whose personality is written into it.

It remains now to say a little on the sources of Locke's ideas and to comment on the style of *Conduct*. The main source of his empiricism lay in his association with the Oxford scientists who were forging new methods of enquiry based on observation and experiment. Especially important was the influence of Robert Boyle, for not only were the two men close friends, but Locke had an intimate knowledge of Boyle's work and shared some of it with him. This influence was reinforced by his own growing interest in medicine and his friendship with the physician Thomas Sydenham. Another source of influence was the French philosopher Gassendi, with whose writings Locke was well acquainted and many of whose views are echoed in the *Essay*.[31] It is evident that his empiricism, in *Conduct* and less noticeably in the *Essay*, is also indebted to Francis Bacon. Locke quotes from the *Magna Instauratio* in the first section of *Conduct*, and there are numerous instances elsewhere of a thoroughly Baconian approach to enquiry; for example in section 24, where Locke makes the same complaint as Bacon against those who indulge in excessive partiality either to the ancients or to the moderns.[32] For further instances the reader should consult the notes in Fowler's edition of *Conduct*. Another major influence, but from a quite different angle, was that of Descartes. This may seem strange, for the spirit of the *Essay* and *Conduct* is far removed from the outlook and methods of Cartesian

[31] See Woozley, *op. cit.*, pp. 11–12.
[32] Sir Francis Bacon, *Novum Organum*, Book I, Aph. 56.

rationalism. Nevertheless, Locke was obviously impressed by the precision and certainty of mathematics (which supplied Descartes' ideal of philosophical method), by its systematic procedure, and by its clear definition of concepts.[33] In fact Locke's conception of knowledge as perception of the agreement or disagreement of ideas is nearer to mathematics than it is to empirical science, and this partly explains his rather grudging inclusion of "sensitive knowledge" within the same epistemological category as intuition and demonstration.

Locke's prose is forthright and vigorous; he states his meaning clearly and directly, rarely wasting words or indulging in needless digression. Perhaps the best adjective to describe his style is "nervous"—in the older meaning, still current in the seventeenth century, of "sinewy," "muscular." This is not to say that his writing lacks interest or is devoid of colour. He expresses himself sometimes with arresting simplicity: "Men see a little, presume a great deal, and so jump to the conclusion." Or again: "We should contend earnestly for the truth, but we should first be sure that it is truth." And: "He that has a mind to believe has half assented already." Sometimes it is the terse, pregnant brevity of his phrasing that compels attention: "Learners must first be believers"; "We are born ignorant of everything." There are also racy passages where his sentences run on with fluent ease from thought to thought, as, for instance, in section 3, where he deplores the narrow vision of those who "canton out to themselves a little Goshen in the intellectual world," or in section 24, where he attacks the prejudice which attributes truth wholly to the ancients or to the moderns. It is true that Locke's sentences are some-

[33] See, for example, *Essay*, IV, iv, 6; and xii, 14 ff.; and *Conduct*, sections 7, 21, 31.

times overlong, occasionally ungrammatical; but his meaning is rarely obscure, and the reader has little difficulty in following the train of his argument. A striking feature of his style is his use of imagery. There is perhaps less of it in *Conduct* than in *Thoughts,* but despite his strictures in section 32, he constantly and often delightfully expresses himself in figurative terms. He writes of men "mewed up within their own contracted territories," of "coffee-house gleaners," of "this court-dresser the fancy," and of making the mind "the warehouse of other men's lumber." He condemns those who read without reflection as merely loading their minds "with a rhapsody of tales fit in winter nights for the entertainment of others." Here and there the imagery is prolonged into a broad sweep of extended figures; examples of this can be found in the sections on Haste and Reasoning.

Locke has managed in *Conduct,* as in his other writings, to combine seriousness of purpose with distinction in style. In brief, it is a readable book, though admittedly it requires effort of the reader; in Locke's own words: "It is seldom that men discover the rich mines without some digging."

BIBLIOGRAPHICAL NOTE

For reasons which a comparison of content and style makes obvious, *Conduct* never achieved the popularity of *Thoughts;* nor has it the importance of the *Essay* or of Locke's political writings. Consequently, there have been fewer editions. The following separate editions are recorded in the British Museum Catalogue and the Library of Congress Catalog:

Some Thoughts on the Conduct of the Understanding in the Search of Truth. London, 1762; also Glasgow, 1763 and 1768.

Some Thoughts on the Conduct of the Understanding in the Search of Truth. A new edition divided under heads. London, 1800; also 1802.

The Conduct of the Understanding in the Search of Truth. A new edition. Edinburgh, 1807.

A Treatise on the Conduct of the Understanding. To which is now added a sketch of his life. A new edition. Boston, 1833; also (apparently the same book), Hartford, Conn., 1851.

Locke's Leitung des Verstandes. Uebersetzt und mit Einleitung herausgegeben, von J. P. Meyer, 1883.

Locke's Conduct of the Understanding, ed. T. Fowler. Oxford, 1881; 5th ed., 1901.

Of the Conduct of the Understanding, ed. A. Louise M. Gilbert, with biography, critical opinions and explanatory notes. New York, 1901.

In a number of editions *Conduct* is combined with *Thoughts,* as, for instance, in J. W. Adamson, *The Educational Writings of John Locke* (Cambridge, 1912, 2nd ed. 1922), and in one with an abstract of the *Essay* (Cambridge, 1781). In some editions it appears with selected writings of Francis Bacon; for example:

Some Thoughts on the Conduct of the Understanding. To which is added Essays moral, economical and political by Francis Bacon, Baron of Verulam. . . . With sketches of the lives of Locke and Bacon. London, 1813.

Students who wish to acquaint themselves with the details of Locke's life should turn to the biography by H. R. Fox Bourne, *The Life of John Locke* (2 vols.; London and New York, 1876) or to that of Maurice Cranston, *John Locke* (London and New York, 1957). The former was long the standard life of Locke and remains a valuable and readable book, although it has now been largely superseded by Cranston's work. This latter incorporates important new material, including much

from the Lovelace collection of Locke's papers, which
was acquired by the Bodleian Library, Oxford, in 1948.
For the Lovelace papers themselves, see P. Long, *A Summary Catalogue of the Lovelace Collection of the Papers
of John Locke in the Bodleian Library* (Oxford, 1959).
Mention should also be made of J. Harrison and P. Laslett, *The Library of John Locke* (Oxford, 1965).

For a general introduction to Locke's philosophical
thought perhaps the best book is R. I. Aaron, *John
Locke* (2nd ed.; Oxford, 1955); but D. J. O'Connor's
John Locke (Harmondsworth, England, 1952) offers a
clear and readable account of his basic thought. An excellent summary may be found in Chapters 4 through 7
of F. Copleston, *A History of Philosophy,* Volume V
(London, 1959). An interesting account of the develop-
ment of Locke's empiricism is given by K. Dewhurst in
John Locke, Physician and Philosopher (London,
1963.) The most recent editions of Locke's *Essay Concerning Human Understanding* are the abridged texts,
edited and introduced by A. D. Woozley (London, 1964)
and by M. Cranston (New York, 1965); another abridged
edition is that of A. S. Pringle-Pattison (Oxford, 1924).
The full text is given in the editions of A. C. Fraser (Oxford, 1894) and J. W. Yolton (2 vols.; London and New
York, 1961).

Locke's political thought is presented in J. W. Gough,
John Locke's Political Philosophy (Oxford, 1950) and,
more recently, in S. P. Lamprecht, *The Moral and Political Philosophy of John Locke* (New York, 1962).
Peter Laslett's edition of the *Two Treatises of Government* (Cambridge, England, 1960) is valuable both for
its introduction and its critical notes. H. R. Penniman,
John Locke on Education and Politics (New York,
1947) has the text of the *Second Treatise of Govern-

ment and of the *Letter Concerning Toleration;* it also contains the only complete text of *Some Thoughts Concerning Education* that is currently in print.

Two abridged editions of *Thoughts* are available: Peter Gay, *John Locke on Education* (New York, 1964) and F. W. Garforth, *Locke's Thoughts Concerning Education* (London and New York, 1964). Earlier editions, now long out of print, are those of R. H. Quick (rev. ed.; Cambridge, England, 1884) and J. W. Adamson, *The Educational Writings of John Locke* (2nd ed.; Cambridge, England, 1922). The latter also includes *Of the Conduct of the Understanding.* Surprisingly little has been written about Locke's educational thought; so far as the present writer is aware, no full critical account of it has yet been published in any English-speaking country; Nina Reicyn's *La pédagogie de John Locke* was published in Paris in 1941. Two major studies are especially needed, one into the sources of Locke's educational thought, the other into its influence in Britain, Europe, and America in the eighteenth century. Numerous articles and essays have appeared; for these the student should consult *The Education Index* (H. W. Wilson, New York) and *The British Education Index* (The Library Association, London.) Separate mention should perhaps be made of R. R. Rusk, *Doctrines of the Great Educators* (3rd ed.; London and New York, 1965), Chapter 7, which contains a number of useful bibliographical references; and P. Nash, A. M. Kazamias, and H. J. Perkinson, *The Educated Man* (London and New York, 1965), Chapter 8.

BRIEF GLOSSARY

A number of the words Locke uses have changed their meaning sufficiently to mislead the modern reader; the most obvious of these are listed hereafter, others are mentioned in the notes:

amuse	mislead, beguile
convenient	fitting, proper
conversation	all kinds of social intercourse (including "conversation" in the modern sense)
indifferent, -ce	impartial, -ity
insignificant	meaningless
nice, -ly	precise, -ly
original	origin (but also as an adjective in the modern sense)
parts	abilities
presently	at once
science	knowledge, branch of knowledge
tract	path, track

Of the Conduct
of the Understanding

A NOTE ON THE TEXT

The text which follows is that of the first edition, posthumously published in 1706. I have modernised the spelling and punctuation and corrected a number of obvious printer's errors; apart from this I have altered the text only when it seemed clearly necessary in order to make sense; these occasions have been very few and are indicated either by brackets (for additions) or in footnotes. There remain, understandably, a number of roughnesses both in grammar and style; these Locke would no doubt have polished out had he been able.

Advertisement To The Reader*

The ensuing treatises are true and genuine remains of the deceased author whose name they bear, but for the greatest part received not his last hand, being in a great measure little more than sudden views, intended to be afterwards revised and further looked into, but by sickness, intervention of business or preferable enquiries happened to be thrust aside and so lay neglected.

The conduct of the understanding he always thought to be a subject very well worth consideration. As any miscarriages in that point accidentally came into his mind, he used sometimes to set them down in writing with those remedies that he could then think of. This method, though it makes not that haste to the end which one could wish, yet perhaps the only one that can be followed in the case. It being here, as in physic, impossible for a physician to describe a disease or seek remedies for it till he comes to meet with it. Such particulars of this kind as occurred to the author at a time of leisure he, as is before said, set down in writing, intending, if he had lived, to have reduced them into order and method and to have made a complete treatise; whereas now it is only a collection of casual observations, sufficient to make men see some faults in the conduct of their understanding and suspect there may be more, and may perhaps serve to excite others to enquire further into it than the author has done.

* This is the original publisher's preface to his volume of Locke's posthumous writings; only the relevant part is printed here. The grammatical irregularities are in the original.

Of the Conduct
of the Understanding

Quid tam temerarium tamque indignum sapientis gravitate atque constantia quam aut falsum sentire aut quod not satis explorate perceptum sit et cognitum sine ulla dubitatione defendere? *

1. *Introduction*. The last resort a man has recourse to in the conduct of himself is his understanding; for though we distinguish the faculties of the mind and give the supreme command to the will as to an agent, yet the truth is, the man which is the agent determines himself to this or that voluntary action upon some precedent knowledge or appearance of knowledge in the understanding.[1] No man ever sets himself about anything but upon some view or other which serves him for a reason for what he does; and whatsoever faculties he employs, the understanding, with such light as it has, well or ill informed, constantly leads; and by that light, true or false, all his operative powers are directed. The will itself, how absolute and uncontrollable soever it may be thought, never fails in its obedience to the dictates of the understanding. Temples have their sacred images,

---

* "What is so reckless and so unworthy of the earnest and unrelenting endeavour of the philosopher than either to hold a false opinion or to maintain unhesitatingly what has been accepted as knowledge without adequate observation and enquiry?"

Cicero, *de Natura Deorum*, Lib. I.

[1] For Locke's account of the will see *Essay*, II, xxi.—F.W.G.

and we see what influence they have always had over a
great part of mankind. But in truth the ideas and images
in men's minds are the invisible powers that constantly
govern them, and to these they all universally pay a
ready submission. It is therefore of the highest concernment that great care should be taken of the understanding to conduct it right in the search of knowledge and
in the judgements it makes.

The logic now in use[2] has so long possessed the chair,
as the only art taught in the schools[3] for the direction of
the mind in the study of the arts and sciences, that it
would perhaps be thought an affectation of novelty to
suspect that rules that have served the learned world
these two or three thousand years and which without any
complaint of defects the learned have rested in are not
sufficient to guide the understanding. And I should not
doubt but this attempt would be censured as vanity or
presumption did not the great Lord Verulam's[4] authority justify it, who, not servilely thinking learning could
not be advanced beyond what it was because for many
ages it had not been, did not rest in the lazy approbation
and applause of what was, because it was, but enlarged
his mind to what might be. In his preface to his *Novum
Organum*[5] concerning logic he pronounces thus, *Qui
summas dialecticae partes tribuerunt atque inde fidis-
sima scientiis praesidia comparari putarunt, verissime*

[2] The scholastic logic derived from Aristotle and based on the
syllogism. Locke makes a strong attack on it in the *Essay*, IV, xvii:
"Syllogism, at best, is but the art of fencing with the little knowledge we have, without making any addition to it."—F.W.G.

[3] That is, of the university (and so regularly in *Conduct*).—F.W.G.

[4] Francis Bacon.—F.W.G.

[5] In fact the passage occurs in the preface to the *Magna Instauratio*, of which the *Novum Organum* was intended to be the second
part.—F.W.G.

*atque optime viderunt intellectum humanum sibi per-
missum merito suspectum esse debere. Verum infirmior
omnino est malo medicina, nec ipsa mali expers. Siqui-
dem dialectica quae recepta est, licet ad civilia et artes
quae in sermone et opinione positae sunt rectissime ad-
hibeatur, naturae tamen subtilitatem longo intervallo
non attingit; et prensando quod non capit ad errores
potius stabiliendos et quasi figendos quam ad viam veri-
tati aperiendam valuit.*

"They," says he, "who attributed so much to logic
perceived very well and truly that it was not safe to trust
the understanding to itself without the guard of any
rules. But the remedy reached not the evil but became a
part of it; for the logic which took place,[6] though it might
do well enough in civil affairs and the arts which consisted in talk and opinion, yet comes very far short of
subtlety in the real performances of nature[7] and, catch-
ing at what it cannot reach, has served to confirm and
establish errors rather than to open a way to truth." And
therefore a little after he says, "That it is absolutely necessary that a better and perfecter use and employment
of the mind and understanding should be introduced."
*Necessario requiritur ut melior et perfectior mentis et
intellectus humani usus et adoperatio introducatur.*

2. *Parts.*[8] There is, it is visible, great variety in men's
understandings, and their natural constitutions put so
wide a difference between some men in this respect that
art and industry would never be able to master, and
their very natures seem to want a foundation to raise on

6 That is, which was received, accepted, in common use.—F.W.G.

7 The point is that syllogistic reasoning, being deductive, is an
inadequate instrument for empirical investigation, which requires
also the use of inductive inference.—F.W.G.

8 Here and regularly in *Conduct* "parts" means "abilities."—
F.W.G.

it that which other men easily attain unto.[9] Amongst men
of equal education there is great inequality of parts. And
the woods of America, as well as the schools of Athens,
produce men of several abilities in the same kind.
Though this be so, yet I imagine most men come very
short of what they might attain unto in their several degrees by a neglect of their understandings. A few rules of
logic are thought sufficient in this case for those who pretend to the highest improvement, whereas I think there
are a great many natural defects in the understanding
capable of amendment which are overlooked and wholly
neglected. And it is easy to perceive that men are guilty
of a great many faults in the exercise and improvement
of this faculty of the mind which hinder them in their
progress and keep them in ignorance and error all their
lives. Some of them I shall take notice of and endeavour to
point out proper remedies for in the following discourse.

3. *Reasoning.* Besides the want of determined ideas[10]
and of sagacity and exercise in finding out and laying in
order intermediate ideas,[11] there are three miscarriages
that men are guilty of in reference to their reason,
whereby this faculty is hindered in them from that service it might do and was designed for. And he that re-
flects upon the actions and discourses of mankind will

[9] Locke was well aware of the power of both heredity and education, and his comments on them suggest, as here, that he was uncertain which was the stronger. See also *Thoughts*, §§ 1, 66, 101–102.
—F.W.G.

[10] See *Essay*, "Epistle to the Reader," and II, xxix; in the former
he writes: "This, I think, may fitly be called a *determinate* or *determined* idea, when, such as it is at any time objectively in the
mind, and so *determined* there, it is annexed and without variation
determined to a name or articulate sound, which is to be steadily
the sign of that very same object of the mind or *determinate* idea."
On the ambiguity of Locke's use of "idea" see the Introduction,
pp. 11–12.—F.W.G.

[11] That is, links in a chain of inference.—F.W.G.

find their defects in this kind very frequent and very observable.

(i) The first is of those who seldom reason at all, but do and think according to the example of others, whether parents, neighbours, ministers or who else they are pleased to make choice of to have an implicit faith in for the saving of themselves the pains and trouble of thinking and examining for themselves.

(ii) The second is of those who put passion in the place of reason and, being resolved that shall govern their actions and arguments, neither use their own nor harken to other people's reason any further than it suits their humour, interest or party; and these, one may observe, commonly content themselves with words which have no distinct ideas to them, though in other matters that they come with an unbiased indifferency to they want not abilities to talk and hear reason, where they have no secret inclination that hinders them from being tractable[12] to it.

(iii) The third sort is of those who readily and sincerely follow reason but, for want of having that which one may call large, sound, roundabout sense, have not a full view of all that relates to the question and may be of moment to decide it. We are all shortsighted and very often see but one side of a matter; our views are not extended to all that has a connection with it. From this defect I think no man is free. We see but in part and we know but in part, and therefore it is no wonder we conclude not right from our partial views. This might instruct the proudest esteemer of his own parts how useful it is to talk and consult with others, even such as came short of him in capacity, quickness and penetra-

[12] The text has "untractable," but this is contrary to the sense. —F.W.G.

tion; for since no one sees all and we generally have different prospects of the same thing according to our different, as I may say, positions to it, it is not incongruous
to think nor beneath any man to try whether another
may not have notions of things which have escaped him
and which his reason would make use of if they came into
his mind. The faculty of reasoning seldom or never de-
ceives those who trust to it; its consequences from what
it builds on are evident and certain; but that which it
oftenest, if not only, misleads us in is that the principles
from which we conclude, the grounds upon which we
bottom our reasoning are but a part; something is left
out which should go into the reckoning to make it just
and exact. Here we may imagine a vast and almost infinite advantage that angels and separate spirits may
have over us, who in their several degrees of elevation
above us may be endowed with more comprehensive
faculties and some of them perhaps have perfect and
exact views of all finite beings that come under their consideration, can, as it were, in the twinkling of an eye collect together all their scattered and almost boundless
relations. A mind so furnished, what reason has it to
acquiesce in the certainty of its conclusions!

In this we may see the reason why some men of study
and thought that reason right and are lovers of truth do
make no great advances in their discoveries of it. Error
and truth are uncertainly blended in their minds; their
decisions are lame and defective, and they are very often
mistaken in their judgements; the reason whereof is,
they converse but with one sort of men, they read but
one sort of books, they will not come in the hearing but
of one sort of notions; the truth is, they canton out to
themselves a little Goshen[13] in the intellectual world

[13] Gen. 47:27.—F.W.G.

where light shines and, as they conclude, day blesses them; but the rest of that vast *expansum* they give up to night and darkness and so avoid coming near it. They have a pretty traffic with known correspondents in some little creek; within that they confine themselves and are dexterous managers enough of the wares and products of that corner with which they content themselves, but will not venture out into the great ocean of knowledge to survey the riches that nature has stored other parts with, no less genuine, no less solid, no less useful than what has fallen to their lot in the admired plenty and sufficiency of their own little spot, which to them contains whatsoever is good in the universe. Those who live thus mewed up within their own contracted territories and will not look abroad beyond the boundaries that chance, conceit or laziness has set to their enquiries, but live separate from the notions, discourses and attainments of the rest of mankind, may not amiss be represented by the inhabitants of the Mariana Islands,[14] which, being separate by a large tract of sea from all communion with the habitable parts of the earth, thought themselves the only people of the world. And though the straitness of the conveniences of life amongst them had never reached so far as to the use of fire till the Spaniards, not many years since, in their voyages from Acapulco to Manilla brought it amongst them, yet in the want and ignorance of almost all things they looked upon themselves, even after that the Spaniards had brought amongst them the notice of variety of nations abounding in sciences, arts and conveniences of life of which they knew nothing, they looked upon themselves, I say, as the happiest and wisest people of the universe. But for all that, nobody,

[14] A group of islands in the western Pacific, also known as the Ladrone Islands.—F.W.G.

I think, will imagine them deep naturalists or solid
metaphysicians; nobody will deem the quickest sighted
amongst them to have very enlarged views in ethics or
politics; nor can anyone allow the most capable amongst
them to be advanced so far in his understanding as to
have any other knowledge but of the few little things of
his and the neighbouring islands within his commerce,[15]
but far enough from that comprehensive enlargement of
mind which adorns a soul devoted to truth, assisted with
letters and a free consideration of the several views and
sentiments of thinking men of all sides. Let not men
therefore that would have a sight of what everyone pretends to be desirous to have a sight of, truth in its full
extent, narrow and blind their own prospect. Let not
men think there is no truth but in the sciences that they
study or the books that they read. To prejudge other
men's notions before we have looked into them is not to
show their darkness but to put out our own eyes. "Try
all things, hold fast that which is good"[16] is a divine rule
coming from the Father of light and truth; and it is hard
to know what other way men may come at truth, to lay
hold of it, if they do not dig and search for it as for gold
and hid treasure; but he that does so must have much
earth and rubbish before he gets the pure metal; sand
and pebbles and dross usually lie blended with it, but
the gold is nevertheless gold and will enrich the man
that employs his pains to seek and separate it. Neither is
there any danger he should be deceived by the mixture.
Every man carries about him a touchstone, if he will
make use of it, to distinguish substantial gold from superficial glitterings, truth from appearances. And indeed
the use and benefit of this touchstone, which is natural

[15] That is, his range of intercourse.—F.W.G.
[16] I Thess. 5:21.—F.W.G.

reason, is spoiled and lost only by assumed prejudices, overweening presumption and narrowing our minds. The want of exercising it in the full extent of things intelligible is that which weakens and extinguishes this noble faculty in us. Trace it and see whether it be not so. The day labourer in a country village has commonly but a small pittance of knowledge because his ideas and notions have been confined to the narrow bounds of a poor conversation and employment; the low mechanic of a country town does somewhat outdo him; porters and cobblers of great cities surpass them. A country gentleman who, leaving Latin and learning in the university, removes thence to his mansion house and associates with neighbours of the same strain, who relish nothing but hunting and a bottle—with those alone he spends his time, with those alone he converses and can away with no company whose discourse goes beyond what claret and dissoluteness inspire. Such a patriot, formed in this happy way of improvement, cannot fail, as we see, to give notable decisions upon the bench at quarter sessions and eminent proofs of his skill in politics, when the strength of his purse and party have advanced him to a more conspicuous station. To such a one truly an ordinary coffee-house gleaner of the city is an errant[17] statesman, and as much superior to, as a man conversant about Whitehall[18] and the Court is to an ordinary shopkeeper. To carry this a little further. Here is one muffled up in the zeal and infallibility of his own

---

[17] J. W. Adamson, *The Educational Writings of John Locke* (2nd ed.; Cambridge, England: 1912), has "arrant," which is a variant form of "errant." An "errant" or "arrant" robber was one who roamed the countryside and was thus well known. The word came to mean "downright," "thorough," "genuine," and did not necessarily carry a pejorative significance.—F.W.G.

[18] The Court was at Whitehall at this time.—F.W.G.

sect and will not touch a book or enter into debate with
a person that will question any of those things which to
him are sacred. Another surveys our differences in religion with an equitable and fair indifference, and so
finds probably that none of them are in everything un-
exceptionable. These divisions and systems were made
by men and carry the mark of fallible on them; and in
those whom he differs from, and till he opened his eyes
had a general prejudice against, he meets with more to
be said for a great many things than before he was aware
of or could have imagined. Which of these two now is
most likely to judge right in our religious controversies
and to be most stored with truth, the mark all pretend to
aim at? All these men that I have instanced in, thus
unequally furnished with truth and advanced in knowledge, I suppose of equal natural parts; all the odds between them has been the different scope that has been
given to their understandings to range in, for the gath-
ering up of information and furnishing their heads with
ideas, notions and observations whereon to employ their
minds and form their understandings.

It will possibly be objected, Who is sufficient for all
this? I answer, more than can be imagined. Everyone
knows what his proper business is and what, according
to the character he makes of himself, the world may
justly expect of him; and to answer that, he will find he
will have time and opportunity enough to furnish himself, if he will not deprive himself by a narrowness of
spirit of those helps that are at hand. I do not say to be
a good geographer that a man should visit every mountain, river, promontory and creek upon the face of the
earth, view the buildings and survey the land everywhere, as if he were going to make a purchase. But yet
everyone must allow that he shall know a country better

that makes often sallies into it and traverses it up and down than he that, like a mill-horse, goes still round in the same tract or keeps within the narrow bounds of a field or two that delight him. He that will enquire out the best books in every science and inform himself of the most material authors of the several sects of philosophy and religion, will not find it an infinite work to acquaint himself with the sentiments of mankind concerning the most weighty and comprehensive subjects. Let him exercise the freedom of his reason and understanding in such a latitude as this, and his mind will be strengthened, his capacity enlarged, his faculties improved; and the light which the remote and scattered parts of truth will give to one another will so assist his judgement, that he will seldom be widely out or miss giving proof of a clear head and a comprehensive knowledge. At least, this is the only way I know to give the understanding its due improvement to the full extent of its capacity, and to distinguish the two most different things I know in the world, a logical chicaner[19] from a man of reason. Only, he that would thus give the mind its flight and send abroad his enquiries into all parts after truth must be sure to settle in his head determined ideas[20] of all that he employs his thoughts about, and never fail to judge himself and judge unbiasedly of all that he receives from others either in their writings or discourses. Reverence or prejudice must not be suffered to give beauty or deformity to any of their opinions.

4. *Of practice and habits.*[21] We are born with faculties and powers capable almost of anything, such at least as

[19] That is, "trickster."—F.W.G.

[20] See footnote 10.—F.W.G.

[21] The importance of practice and habit is a constant theme of *Thoughts,* for instance, in §§ 66 and 107.—F.W.G.

would carry us further than can be easily imagined; but it is only the exercise of those powers which gives us ability and skill in anything and leads us towards perfection.

A middle-aged ploughman will scarce ever be brought to the carriage and language of a gentleman, though his body be as well proportioned and his joints as supple and his natural parts not any way inferior. The legs of a dancing-master and the fingers of a musician fall as it were naturally without thought or pains into regular and admirable motions. Bid them change their parts, and they will in vain endeavour to produce like motions in the members not used to them, and it will require length of time and long practice to attain but some degrees of a like ability. What incredible and astonishing actions do we find rope-dancers and tumblers bring their bodies to——not but that sundry in almost all manual arts are as wonderful, but I name those which the world takes notice of for such, because on that very account they give money to see them. All these admired motions beyond the reach and almost the conception of unpractised spectators are nothing but the mere effects of use and industry in men whose bodies have nothing peculiar in them from those of the amazed lookers on.

As it is in the body, so it is in the mind; practice makes it what it is, and most even of those excellences which are looked on as natural endowments will be found, when examined into more narrowly, to be the product of exercise and to be raised to that pitch only by repeated actions. Some men are remarked for pleasantness in raillery, others for apologues[22] and apposite diverting stories. This is apt to be taken for the effect of pure nature,

---

[22] An allegorical story conveying a lesson or moral.—F.W.G.

and that the rather, because it is not got by rules, and those who excel in either of them never purposely set themselves to the study of it as an art to be learnt. But yet it is true that at first some lucky hit, which took with somebody and gained him commendation, encouraged him to try again, inclined his thoughts and endeavours that way, till at last he insensibly got a facility in it without perceiving how, and that is attributed wholly to nature which was much more the effect of use and practice. I do not deny that natural disposition may often give the first rise to it; but that never carries a man far without use and exercise, and it is practice alone that brings the powers of the mind as well as those of the body to their perfection. Many a good poetic vein is buried under a trade and never produces anything for want of improvement. We see the ways of discourse and reasoning are very different, even concerning the same matter, at Court and in the university. And he that will go but from Westminster Hall to the Exchange[23] will find a different genius and turn in their ways of talking, and yet one cannot think that all whose lot fell in the City were born with different parts from those who were bred at the university or Inns of Court.

To what purpose all this but to show that the difference so observable in men's understandings and parts does not arise so much from their natural faculties as acquired habits. He would be laughed at that should go about to make a fine dancer out of a country hedger at past fifty; and he will not have much better success who shall endeavour at that age to make a man reason well or speak handsomely who has never been used to it, though you should lay before him a collection of all

[23] That is, from the Law Courts to the Royal Exchange, London's financial centre.—F.W.G.

the best precepts of logic or oratory. Nobody is made anything by hearing of rules or laying them up in his memory; practice must settle the habit of doing without reflecting on the rule, and you may as well hope to make a good painter or musician extempore by a lecture and instruction in the arts of music and painting as a coherent thinker or strict reasoner by a set of rules showing him wherein right reasoning consists.

This being so, that defects and weaknesses in men's understandings, as well as other faculties, come from want of a right use of their own minds, I am apt to think the fault is generally mislaid upon nature and there is often a complaint of want of parts when the fault lies in want of a due improvement of them. We see men frequently dexterous and sharp enough in making a bargain who, if you reason with them about matters of religion, appear perfectly stupid.

5. *Idea*s. I will not here, in what relates to the right conduct and improvement of the understanding, repeat again the getting clear and determined ideas and the employing our thoughts rather about them than about sounds put for them, nor of settling the signification of words which we use with ourselves in the search of truth or with others in discoursing about it. Those hindrances of our understandings in the pursuit of knowledge I have sufficiently enlarged upon in another place,[24] so that nothing more needs here to be said of those matters.

6. *Principles*. There is another fault that stops or misleads men in their knowledge, which I have also spoken something of but yet is necessary to mention here again, that we may examine it to the bottom and see the root it springs from, and that is a custom of taking up with

---

[24] That is, in *Essay*, III, especially ix–xi.

principles[25] that are not self-evident and very often not so much true. It is not unusual to see men rest their opinions upon foundations that have no more certainty nor solidity than the propositions built on them and embraced for their sake. Such foundations are these and the like, viz.: the founders or leaders of my party are good men and therefore their tenets are true; it is the opinion of a sect that is erroneous, therefore it is false; it has been long received in the world, therefore it is true; or it is new, and therefore false.

These and many the like, which are by no means the measures of truth and falsehood, the generality of men make the standards by which they accustom their understanding to judge. And thus they falling into a habit of determining of truth and falsehood by such wrong measures, it is no wonder they should embrace error for certainty and be very positive in things they have no ground for.

There is not any who pretends to the least reason but, when any of these his false maxims are brought to the test, must acknowledge them to be fallible and such as he will not allow in those that differ from him; and yet after he is convinced of this you shall see him go on in the use of them and the very next occasion that offers argue again upon the same grounds. Would one not be ready to think that men are willing to impose upon themselves and mislead their own understanding who conduct them by such wrong measures even after they see they cannot be relied on? But yet they will not appear so blameable as may be thought at first sight; for I think there are a great many that argue thus in earnest and do it not to impose on themselves or others. They are persuaded of

[25] That is, arguing from premisses. On this subject see also *Essay*, IV, xx, especially 8–10.—F.W.G.

what they say and think there is weight in it, though in a
like case they have been convinced there is none; but
men would be intolerable to themselves and contemptible to others, if they should embrace opinions without
any ground and hold what they could give no manner of
reason for. True or false, solid or sandy, the mind must
have some foundation to rest itself upon, and, as I have
remarked in another place,[26] it no sooner entertains any
proposition but it presently hastens to some hypothesis
to bottom it on; till then it is unquiet and unsettled. So
much do our own very tempers dispose us to a right use
of our understandings, if we would follow as we should
the inclinations of our nature.

In some matters of concernment, especially those of
religion, men are not permitted to be always wavering
and uncertain; they must embrace and profess some
tenets or other; and it would be a shame, nay a contra-
diction, too heavy for anyone's mind to lie constantly
under, for him to pretend seriously to be persuaded of
the truth of any religion and yet not to be able to give
any reason of one's belief or to say anything for his preference of this to any other opinion. And therefore they
must make use of some principles or other, and those can
be no other than such as they have and can manage; and
to say they are not in earnest persuaded by them and do
not rest upon those they make use of, is contrary to experience and to allege that they are not misled when we
complain they are.

If this be so, it will be urged, why then do they not
rather make use of sure and unquestionable principles
rather than rest on such grounds as may deceive them
and will, as is visible, serve to support error as well as
truth?

[26] *Essay*, IV, xii, 12–13.—F.W.G.

To this I answer, the reason why they do not make use of better and surer principles is because they cannot; but this inability proceeds not from want of natural parts (for those few whose case that is are to be excused) but for want of use and exercise. Few men are from their youth accustomed to strict reasoning and to trace the dependence of any truth in a long train of consequences to its remote principles and to observe its connection; and he that by frequent practice has not been used to this employment of his understanding, it is no more wonder that he should not, when he is grown into years, be able to bring his mind to it, than that he should not be on a sudden able to grave or design, dance on the ropes, or write a good hand who has never practised either of them.

Nay, the most of men are so wholly strangers to this, that they do not so much as perceive their want of it. They dispatch the ordinary business of their callings by rote, as we say, as they have learnt it, and if at any time they miss success, they impute it to anything rather than want of thought or skill; that they conclude (because they know no better) they have in perfection. Or if there be any subject that interest or fancy has recommended to their thoughts, their reasoning about it is still after their own fashion; be it better or worse, it serves their turns and is the best they are acquainted with; and therefore when they are led by it into mistakes and their business succeeds accordingly, they impute it to any cross accident or default of others rather than to their own want of understanding; that is what nobody discovers or complains of in himself. Whatsoever made his business to miscarry, it was not want of right thought and judgement in himself; he sees no such defect in himself, but is satisfied that he carries on his designs well enough by his own reasoning, or at least should have done, had it not been for unlucky traverses[27] not in his power. Thus being content with this short and very imperfect use of his understanding, he never troubles himself to seek out methods of improving his mind, and lives all his life without any notion of close reasoning in a continued connection of a long train of consequences from sure foundations, such as is requisite for the making out and clearing most of the speculative truths most men own to believe and are most concerned in. Not to mention here what I shall have occasion to insist on by and by more fully,[28] viz., that in many cases it is not one series of consequences will serve the turn, but many different and opposite deductions must be examined and laid together before a man can come to make a right judgement of the point in question. What then can be expected from men that neither see the want of any such kind of reasoning as this nor, if they do, know they how to set about it or could perform it? You may as well set a countryman who scarce knows the figures and never cast up a sum of three particulars to state a merchant's long account and find the true balance of it.

What then should be done in the case? I answer, we should always remember what I said above, that the faculties of our souls are improved and made useful to us just after the same manner as our bodies are. Would you have a man write or paint, dance or fence well, or perform any other manual operation dexterously and with ease, let him have never so much vigour and activity, suppleness and address naturally, yet nobody expects this from him unless he has been used to it and has employed time and pains in fashioning and forming

27 That is, "obstructions."—F.W.G.
28 That is, in the next section.—F.W.G.

his hand or outward parts to these motions. Just so it is in the mind; would you have a man reason well, you must use him to it betimes, exercise his mind in observing the connection of ideas and following them in train. Nothing does this better than mathematics, which therefore I think should be taught all those who have the time and opportunity, not so much to make them mathematicians as to make them reasonable creatures;[29] for though we all call ourselves so, because we are born to it if we please, yet we may truly say nature gives us but the seeds of it; we are born to be, if we please, rational creatures, but it is use and exercise only that makes us so, and we are indeed so no further than industry and application has carried us. And therefore in ways of reasoning which men have not been used to, he that will observe the conclusions they take up must be satisfied they are not all rational.

This has been the less taken notice of, because everyone in his private affairs uses some sort of reasoning or other, enough to denominate him reasonable. But the mistake is that he that is found reasonable in one thing is concluded to be so in all, and to think or say otherwise is thought so unjust an affront and so senseless a censure that nobody ventures to do it. It looks like the degradation of a man below the dignity of his nature. It is true, that he that reasons well in any one thing has a mind naturally capable of reasoning well in others, and to the same degree of strength and clearness, and possibly much greater, had his understanding been so employed. But it is as true that he who can reason well today

29 Locke's proposal assumes that training acquired within one subject can either be transferred to others or generalised into principles of intellectual activity; in fact this is possible only within fairly narrow limits.—F.W.G.

about one sort of matters cannot at all reason today about others, though perhaps a year hence he may. But wherever a man's rational faculty fails him and will not serve him to reason, there we cannot say he is rational, how capable soever he may be by time and exercise to become so.

Try in men of low and mean education, who have never elevated their thoughts above the spade and the plough nor looked beyond the ordinary drudgery of a day-labourer. Take the thoughts of such an one, used for many years to one tract, out of that narrow compass he has been all his life confined to, you will find him no more capable of reasoning than almost a perfect natural. Some one or two rules on which their conclusions immediately depend you will find in most men have governed all their thoughts; these, true or false, have been the maxims they have been guided by. Take these from them, and they are perfectly at a loss, their compass and polestar then are gone and their understanding is perfectly at a nonplus; and therefore they either immediately return to their old maxims again as the foundations of all truth to them, notwithstanding all that can be said to show their weakness, or, if they give them up to their reasons, they with them give up all truth and further enquiry and think there is no such thing as certainty. For if you would enlarge their thoughts and settle them upon more remote and surer principles, they either cannot easily apprehend them, or, if they can, know not what use to make of them; for long deductions from remote principles is what they have not been used to and cannot manage.

What then, can grown men never be improved or enlarged in their understandings? I say not so, but this I think I may say, that it will not be done without industry and application, which will require more time and pains than grown men, settled in their course of life, will allow to it, and therefore very seldom is done. And this very capacity of attaining it by use and exercise only brings us back to that which I laid down before, that it is only practice that improves our minds as well as bodies, and we must expect nothing from our understandings any further than they are perfected by habits.

The Americans are not all born with worse understandings than the Europeans, though we see none of them have such reaches in the arts and sciences. And among the children of a poor countryman the lucky chance of education and getting into the world gives one infinitely the superiority in parts over the rest, who, continuing at home, had continued also just of the same size with his brethren.

He that has to do with young scholars, especially in mathematics, may perceive how their minds open by degrees, and how it is exercise alone that opens them. Sometimes they will stick a long time at a part of a demonstration, not for want of will or application, but really for want of perceiving the connection of two ideas that, to one whose understanding is more exercised, is as visible as anything can be. The same would be with a grown man beginning to study mathematics; the understanding, for want of use, often sticks in very plain way, and he himself that is so puzzled, when he comes to see the connection, wonders what it was he stuck at in a case so plain.

7. *Mathematics.* I have mentioned mathematics as a way to settle in the mind a habit of reasoning closely and in train; not that I think it necessary that all men should be deep mathematicians, but that having got the way of reasoning, which that study necessarily brings the mind

to, they might be able to transfer it to other parts of
knowledge as they shall have occasion.[30] For in all sorts
of reasoning every single argument should be managed
as a mathematical demonstration; the connection and
dependence of ideas should be followed till the mind
is brought to the source on which it bottoms and observes
the coherence all along, though in proofs of probability
one such train is not enough to settle the judgement as
in demonstrative knowledge.[31]

Where a truth is made out by one demonstration, there
needs no further enquiry; but in probabilities, where
there wants demonstration to establish the truth beyond
doubt, there it is not enough to trace one argument to
its source and observe its strength and weakness, but all
the arguments, after having been so examined on both
sides, must be laid in balance one against another, and
upon the whole the understanding determine its assent.

This is a way of reasoning the understanding should
be accustomed to, which is so different from what the
illiterate are used to that even learned men oftentimes
seem to have very little or no notion of it. Nor is it to
be wondered, since the way of disputing in the schools
leads them quite away from it by insisting on one topical argument,[32] by the success of which the truth or falsehood of the question is to be determined and victory
adjudged to the opponent or defendant; which is all
one as if one should balance an account by one sum
charged and discharged, when there are a hundred
others to be taken into consideration.

[30] See footnote 29.—F.W.G.

[31] See Introduction, pp. 9–10. For Locke's account of probability,
see *Essay*, IV, xv, xvi, and xx.—F.W.G.

[32] Locke refers to the formal disputations which were regularly
practised in the universities of his time. By "one topical argument"

This therefore it would be well if men's minds were accustomed to, and that early, that they might not erect their opinions upon one single view, when so many other are requisite to make up the account and must come into the reckoning before a man can form a right judgement. This would enlarge their minds and give a due freedom to their understandings, that they might not be led into error by presumption, laziness or precipitancy; for I think nobody can approve such a conduct of the understanding as should mislead it from truth, though it be never so much in fashion to make use of it.

To this perhaps it will be objected that to manage the understanding as I propose would require every man to be a scholar and to be furnished with all the materials of knowledge and exercised in all the ways of reasoning. To which I answer that it is a shame for those that have time and the means to attain knowledge to want any helps or assistance for the improvement of their under-standings that are to be got, and to such I would be thought here chiefly to speak. Those, methinks, who by the industry and parts of their ancestors have been set free from a constant drudgery to their backs and their bellies, should bestow some of their spare time on their heads and open their minds by some trials and essays in all the sorts and matters of reasoning. I have before mentioned mathematics, wherein algebra gives new helps and views to the understanding. If I propose these, it is not, as I said, to make every man a thorough mathe-matician or a deep algebraist; but yet I think the study of them is of infinite use even to grown men. First, by exper-imentally convincing them that to make anyone reason

he means an argument restricted to a single "topic" or general prin-ciple. See *Essay*, IV, xvii, 5.—F.W.G.

well it is not enough to have parts wherewith he is satisfied and that serve him well enough in his ordinary
course. A man in those studies will see that, however
good he may think his understanding, yet in many
things, and those very visible, it may fail him. This would
take off that presumption that most men have of themselves in this part; and they would not be so apt to think
their minds wanted no helps to enlarge them, that
there could be nothing added to the acuteness and
penetration of their understandings.

Secondly, the study of mathematics would show them
the necessity there is in reasoning to separate all the
distinct ideas and see the habitudes[33] that all those
concerned in the present enquiry have to one another,
and to lay by those which relate not to the proposition
in hand and wholly to leave them out of the reckoning.
This is that which in other subjects besides quantity[34] is
what is absolutely requisite to just reasoning, though in
them it is not so easily observed nor so carefully practised.
In those parts of knowledge where it is thought demonstration has nothing to do, men reason as it were in the
lump; and if, upon a summary and confused view or
upon a partial consideration, they can raise the appearance of a probability, they usually rest content, especially
if it be in a dispute where every little straw is laid hold
on and everything that can but be drawn in any way to
give colour to the argument is advanced with ostentation. But that mind is not in a posture to find the truth
that does not distinctly take all the parts asunder and,
omitting what is not at all to the point, draw a conclusion from the result of all the particulars which any way

[33] That is, "relationships," "dispositions" (as also in sections 15,
19, 26, etc.).—F.W.G.
[34] That is, besides mathematics.—F.W.G.

influence it. There is another no less useful habit to be got by an application to mathematical demonstrations, and that is of using[35] the mind to a long train of consequences; but having mentioned that already[36] I shall not again here repeat it.

As to men whose fortunes and time is narrower, what may suffice them is not of that vast extent as may be imagined, and so comes not within the objection.

Nobody is under an obligation to know everything. Knowledge and science in general is the business only of those who are at ease and leisure. Those who have particular callings ought to understand them; and it is no unreasonable proposal, nor impossible to be compassed, that they should think and reason right about what is their daily employment. This one cannot think them incapable of without levelling them with the brutes and charging them with a stupidity below the rank of rational creatures.

8. *Religion.* Besides his particular calling for the support of his life, everyone has a concern in a future life which he is bound to look after. This engages his thoughts in religion; and here it mightily lies upon him to understand and reason right. Men therefore cannot be excused from understanding the words and framing the general notions relating to religion right. The one day of seven, besides other days of rest, allows in the Christian world time enough for this (had they no other idle hours) if they would but make use of these vacancies from their daily labour and apply themselves to an improvement of knowledge with as much diligence as they often do to a great many other things that are useless, and had but those that would enter them according to

35 That is, "accustoming."—F.W.G.
36 That is, in the previous section.—F.W.G.

their several capacities in a right way to this knowledge. The original make of their minds is like that of other men, and they would be found not to want understanding fit to receive the knowledge of religion, if they were a little encouraged and helped in it as they should be. For there are instances of very mean people who have raised their minds to a great sense and understanding of religion. And though these have not been so frequent as could be wished, yet they are enough to clear that condition of life from a necessity of gross ignorance and to show that more might be brought to be rational creatures and Christians (for they can hardly be thought really to be so who, wearing the name, know not so much as the very principles of that religion) if due care were taken of them. For, if I mistake not, the peasantry lately in France (a rank of people under a much heavier pressure of want and poverty than the day-labourers in England) of the reformed religion understood it much better and could say more for it than those of a higher condition among us.[37]

But if it shall be concluded that the meaner sort of people must give themselves up to a brutish stupidity in the things of their nearest concernment, which I see no reason for, this excuses not those of a freer fortune and education, if they neglect their understandings and take no care to employ them as they ought and set them right in the knowledge of those things for which principally they were given them. At least those whose plentiful fortunes allow them the opportunities and helps of improvements are not so few but that it might be hoped

---

[37] Locke is writing from personal experience here as a result of his travels in France. He refers to the French Protestants or Huguenots, who in 1685 had been deprived of their civil and religious liberties by the revocation of the Edict of Nantes.—F.W.G.

great advancements might be made in knowledge of all kinds, especially in that of the greatest concern and largest views, if men would make a right use of their faculties and study their own understandings.

9. *Ideas*. Outward corporeal objects that constantly importune our senses and captivate our appetites fail not to fill our heads with lively and lasting ideas of that kind. Here the mind needs not be set upon getting greater store; they offer themselves fast enough and are usually entertained in such plenty and lodged so carefully, that the mind wants room or attention for others that it has more use and need of. To fit the understanding therefore for such reasoning as I have been above speaking of, care should be taken to fill it with moral and more abstract ideas; for these not offering themselves to the senses, but being to be framed to the understanding, people are generally so neglectful of a faculty they are apt to think wants nothing, that I fear most men's minds are more unfurnished with such ideas than is imagined. They often use the words, and how can they be suspected to want the ideas? What I have said in the third book of my essay will excuse me from any other answer to this question. But to convince people of what moment it is to their understandings to be furnished with such abstract ideas steady and settled in it, give me leave to ask how anyone shall be able to know whether he be obliged to be just, if he has not established ideas in his mind of obligation and of justice, since knowledge consists in nothing but the perceived agreement or disagreement of those ideas;[38] and so of all

[38] This is the definition of knowledge which Locke proposes in *Essay*, IV, i, 2: "Knowledge then seems to me to be nothing but the perception of the connexion and agreement, or disagreement and repugnancy, of any of our ideas. In this alone it consists."—F.W.G.

others the like which concern our lives and manners.
And if men do find a difficulty to see the agreement or
disagreement of two angles which lie before their eyes,
unalterable in a diagram, how utterly impossible will
it be to perceive it in ideas that have no other sensible
objects to represent them to the mind but sounds, with
which they have no manner of conformity and therefore
had need to be clearly settled in the mind themselves if
we would make any clear judgement about them. This,
therefore, is one of the first things the mind should be
employed about in the right conduct of the understanding, without which it is impossible it should be capable
of reasoning right about those matters. But in these and
all other ideas care must be taken that they harbour no
inconsistencies, and that they have a real existence where
real existence is supposed and are not mere chimeras
with a supposed existence.

10. *Prejudice.* Everyone is forward to complain of the
prejudices that mislead other men or parties, as if he
were free and had none of his own. This being objected
on all sides, it is agreed that it is a fault and a hindrance
to knowledge. What now is the cure? No other but this,
that every man should let alone others' prejudices and
examine his own. Nobody is convinced of his by the
accusation of another; he recriminates by the same rule
and is clear. The only way to remove this great cause of
ignorance and error out of the world is for everyone im-
partially to examine himself. If others will not deal
fairly with their own minds, does that make my errors
truths, or ought it to make me in love with them and
willing to impose on myself? If others love cataracts
on their eyes, should that hinder me from couching of
mine as soon as I could? Everyone declares against
blindness, and yet who almost is not fond of that which

dims his sight and keeps the clear light out of his mind, which should lead him into truth and knowledge? False or doubtful positions, relied upon as unquestionable maxims, keep those in the dark from truth who build on them. Such are usually the prejudices imbibed from education, party, reverence, fashion, interest, etc. This is the mote which everyone sees in his brother's eye, but never regards the beam in his own. For who is there almost that is ever brought fairly to examine his own principles and see whether they are such as will bear the trial? But yet this should be one of the first things everyone should set about and be scrupulous in, who would rightly conduct his understanding in the search of truth and knowledge.

To those who are willing to get rid of this great hindrance of knowledge (for to such only I write), to those who would shake off this great and dangerous impostor, prejudice, who dresses up falsehood in the likeness of truth and so dexterously hoodwinks men's minds as to keep them in the dark with a belief that they are more in the light than any that do not see with their eyes, I shall offer this one mark whereby prejudice may be known. He that is strongly of any opinion must suppose (unless he be self-condemned) that his persuasion is built upon good grounds, and that his assent is no greater than what the evidence of the truth he holds forces him to, and that they are arguments, and not inclination or fancy, that make him so confident and positive in his tenets. Now if, after all his profession, he cannot bear any opposition to his opinion, if he cannot so much as give a patient hearing, much less examine and weigh the arguments on the other side, does he not plainly confess it is prejudice governs him and it is not the evidence of truth, but some lazy anticipation, some beloved pre-

sumption that he desires to rest undisturbed in? For if
what he holds be as he give out, well fenced with evidence, and he sees it to be true, what need he fear to put
it to the proof? If his opinion be settled upon a firm
foundation, if the arguments that support it and have
obtained his assent be clear, good and convincing, why
should he be shy to have it tried whether they be proof
or not? He whose assent goes beyond his evidence owes
this excess of his adherence only to prejudice and does,
in effect, own it when he refuses to hear what is offered
against it, declaring thereby that it is not evidence he
seeks, but the quiet enjoyment of the opinion he is
fond of, with a forward condemnation of all that
may stand in opposition to it, unheard and unexamined;
which, what is it but prejudice? *Qui aequum statuerit
parte inaudita altera, etiam si aequum statuerit, haud
aequus fuerit.*[39] He that would acquit himself in this
case as a lover of truth, not giving way to any preoccupa-
tion or bias that may mislead him, must do two things
that are not very common nor very easy.

11. *Indifferency.* First, he must not be in love with any
opinion or wish it to be true till he knows it to be so,
and then he will not need to wish it. For nothing that is
false can deserve our good wishes nor a desire that it
should have the place and force of truth; and yet nothing is more frequent than this. Men are fond of certain
tenets upon no other evidence but respect and custom,
and think they must maintain them or all is gone,
though they have never examined the ground they stand
on, nor have ever made them out to themselves or can

[39] "A man who decides a case after hearing only one side of it
cannot himself be called just, even though the decision is just." A
sentence very similar to this occurs in Seneca's *Medea*, ll. 199–200.
—F.W.G.

make them out to others. We should contend earnestly for the truth, but we should first be sure that it is truth, or else we fight against God, who is the God of truth, and do the work of the devil, who is the father and propagator of lies; and our zeal, though never so warm, will not excuse us; for this is plainly prejudice.

12. *Examine.* Secondly, he must do that which he will find himself very averse to, as judging the thing unnecessary or himself incapable of doing it. He must try whether his principles be certainly true or not, and how far he may safely rely upon them. This, whether fewer have the heart or the skill to do, I shall not determine; but this I am sure, this is that which everyone ought to do who professes to love truth and would not impose upon himself—which is a surer way to be made a fool of than by being exposed to the sophistry of others. The disposition to put any cheat upon ourselves works constantly and we are pleased with it, but are impatient of being bantered or misled by others. The inability I here speak of is not any natural defect that makes men incapable of examining their own principles. To such, rules of conducting their understandings are useless, and that is the case of very few. The great number is of those whom the ill habit of never exerting their thoughts has disabled; the powers of their minds are starved by disuse and have lost that reach and strength which nature fitted them to receive from exercise. Those who are in a condition to learn the first rules of plain arithmetic and could be brought to cast up an ordinary sum are capable of this, if they had but accustomed their minds to reasoning; but they that have wholly neglected the exercise of their understandings in this way will be very far at first from being able to do it and as unfit for it as one unpractised in figures to cast up a shop-book, and

perhaps think it as strange to be set about it. And yet it
must nevertheless be confessed to be a wrong use of our
understandings to build our tenets (in things where we
are concerned to hold the truth) upon principles that
may lead us into error. We take our principles at haphazard upon trust and without ever having examined
them, and then believe a whole system upon a presumption that they are true and solid. And what is all this but
childish, shameful, senseless credulity?

In these two things, viz., an equal indifferency for all
truth (I mean the receiving it in the love of it as truth,
but not loving it for any other reason before we know
it to be true) and in the examination of our principles
and not receiving any for such nor building on them till
we are fully convinced, as rational creatures, of their
solidity, truth and certainty, consists that freedom of
the understanding which is necessary to a rational creature and without which it is not truly an understanding.
It is conceit, fancy, extravagance, anything rather than
understanding, if it must be under the constraint of
receiving and holding opinions by the authority of anything but their own, not fancied but perceived, evidence.
This was rightly called imposition, and is of all other the
worst and most dangerous sort of it. For we impose upon
ourselves, which is the strongest imposition of all others,
and we impose upon ourselves in that part which ought
with the greatest care to be kept free from all imposition.
The world is apt to cast great blame on those who have
an indifferency for opinions, especially in religion. I
fear this is the foundation of great error and worse
consequences. To be indifferent which of two opinions is
true is the right temper of the mind that preserves it from
being imposed on and disposes it to examine with that
indifferency till it has done its best to find the truth;

and this is the only direct and safe way to it. But to be indifferent whether we embrace falsehood for truth or no is the great road to error. Those who are not indifferent which opinion is true are guilty of this; they suppose, without examining, that what they hold is true and then think they ought to be zealous for it. Those, it is plain by their warmth and eagerness, are not indifferent for their own opinions, but methinks are very indifferent whether they be true or false, since they cannot endure to have any doubts raised or objections made against them; and it is visible they never have made any themselves, and so, never having examined them, know not nor are concerned, as they should be, to know whether they be true or false.

These are the common and most general miscarriages which I think men should avoid or rectify in a right conduct of their understandings, and should be particularly taken care of in education. The business whereof in respect of knowledge is not, as I think, to perfect a learner in all or any one of the sciences, but to give his mind that freedom, that disposition and those habits that may enable him to attain any part of knowledge he shall apply himself to or stand in need of in the future course of his life.[40]

This and this only is well principling, and not the

---

[40] Compare *Thoughts*, § 94: "The great work of a governor [i.e. tutor] is to fashion the carriage and form the mind; to settle in his pupil good habits and the principles of virtue and wisdom; to give by little and little a view of mankind, and work him into a love and imitation of what is excellent and praiseworthy; and in the prosecution of it to give him vigour, activity and industry. The studies which he sets him on are but, as it were, the exercises of his faculties and employment of his time, to keep him from sauntering and idleness, to teach him application and accustom him to take pains, and to give him some little taste of what his own industry must perfect."—F.W.G.

instilling a reverence and veneration for certain dogmas
under the specious title of principles, which are often so
remote from that truth and evidence which belongs to
principles, that they ought to be rejected as false and
erroneous; and is often the cause to men so educated,
when they come abroad into the world and find they
cannot maintain the principles so taken up and rested
in, to cast off all principles and turn perfect sceptics,
regardless of knowledge and virtue.

There are several weaknesses and defects in the understanding, either from the natural temper of the mind or
ill habits taken up, which hinder it in its progress to
knowledge. Of these there are as many possibly to be
found, if the mind were thoroughly studied, as there are
diseases of the body, each whereof clogs and disables
the understanding to some degree and therefore deserves to be looked after and cured. I shall set down
some few to excite men, especially those who make
knowledge their business, to look into themselves and observe whether they do not indulge some weakness, allow
some miscarriages in the management of their intellectual faculty, which is prejudicial to them in the search
for truth.

13. *Observation.* Particular matters of fact are the un-
doubted foundations on which our civil and natural
knowledge is built; the benefit the understanding makes
of them is to draw from them conclusions which may be
as standing rules of knowledge and consequently of practice. The mind often makes not that benefit it should of
the information it receives from the accounts of civil
or natural historians, in being too forward or too slow
in making observations on the particular facts recorded
in them.

There are those who are very assiduous in reading

and yet do not much advance their knowledge by it. They are delighted with the stories that are told and perhaps can tell them again, for they make all they read nothing but history[41] to themselves; but not reflecting on it, not making to themselves observations from what they read, they are very little improved by all that crowd of particulars that either pass through or lodge themselves in their understandings. They dream on in a constant course of reading and cramming themselves; but, not digesting anything, it produces nothing but a heap of crudities.

If their memories retain well, one may say they have the materials of knowledge, but, like those for building, they are of no advantage if there be no other use made of them but to let them lie heaped up together. Opposite to these there are others who lose the improvement they should make of matters of fact by a quite contrary conduct. They are apt to draw general conclusions and raise axioms from every particular they meet with. These make as little true benefit of history as the other, nay, being of forward and active spirits receive more harm by it; it being of worse consequence to steer one's thoughts by a wrong rule than to have none at all, error doing to busy men much more harm than ignorance to the slow and sluggish. Between these, those seem to do best who, taking material and useful hints, sometimes from single matters of fact, carry them in their minds to be judged of by what they shall find in history to confirm or reverse these imperfect observations; which may be established into rules fit to be relied on when they are justified by a sufficient and wary induction of

41 That is, a mere record of facts or events. The word "history" in Locke's time could mean a systematic record of facts in any field of knowledge.—F.W.G.

particulars.[42] He that makes no such reflections on what
he reads only loads his mind with a rhapsody of tales
fit in winter nights for the entertainment of others; and
he that will improve every matter of fact into a maxim
will abound in contrary observations that can be of no
other use but to perplex and pudder[43] him if he com-
pares them; or else to misguide him, if he gives himself
up to the authority of that which, for its novelty or for
some other fancy, best pleases him.

14. *Bias.* Next to these we may place those who suffer
their own natural tempers and passions they are possessed with to influence their judgements, especially of
men and things that may any way relate to their present
circumstances and interest. Truth is all simple, all pure,
will bear no mixture of anything else with it. It is rigid
and inflexible to any by-interests; and so should the
understanding be, whose use and excellency lies in con-
forming itself to it. To think of everything just as it is in
itself is the proper business of the understanding, though
it be not that which men always employ it to. This all
men, at first hearing, allow is the right use everyone
should make of his understanding. Nobody will be at
such an open defiance with common sense as to profess
that we should not endeavour to know and think of
things as they are in themselves, and yet there is nothing
more frequent than to do the contrary; and men are apt
to excuse themselves, and think they have reason to do
so, if they have but a pretence that it is for God or a
good cause, that is, in effect, for themselves, their own
persuasion or party; for those in their turns the several
sects of men, especially in matters of religion, entitle God

[42] That is, by an inductive argument from particular facts to general truths.—F.W.G.
[43] That is, "confuse" (the derivation is uncertain).—F.W.G.

and a good cause. But God requires not men to wrong or misuse their faculties for him, nor to lie to others or themselves for his sake; which they purposely do who will not suffer their understandings to have right conceptions of the things proposed to them and designedly restrain themselves from having just thoughts of everything, as far as they are concerned to enquire. And as for a good cause, that needs not such ill helps; if it be good, truth will support it and it has no need of fallacy or falsehood.

15. *Arguments.* Very much of kin to this is the hunting after arguments to make good one side of a question and wholly to neglect and refuse those which favour the other side. What is this but wilfully to misguide the understanding (and is so far from giving truth its due value that it wholly debases it), [to] espouse opinions that best comport with their power, profit or credit and then seek arguments to support them? Truth lighted upon this way is of no more avail to us than error; for what is so taken up by us may be false as well as true, and he has not done his duty who has thus stumbled upon truth in his way to preferment.

There is another but more innocent way of collecting arguments, very familiar among bookish men, which is to furnish themselves with the arguments they meet with pro and con in the questions they study. This helps them not to judge right nor argue strongly, but only to talk copiously on either side, without being steady and settled in their own judgements; for such arguments gathered from other men's thoughts, floating only in the memory, are there ready indeed to supply copious talk with some appearance of reason, but are far from helping us to judge right. Such variety of arguments only distract the understanding that relies on them, unless it has gone further than such a superficial way of examining; this is to quit truth for appearance, only to serve our vanity. The sure and only way to get true knowledge is to form in our minds clear settled notions of things, with names annexed to those determined ideas.[44] These we are to consider, and with their several relations and habitudes,[45] and not to amuse ourselves with floating names and words of indetermined signification, which we can use in several senses to serve a turn. It is in the perception of the habitudes and respects our ideas have one to another that real knowledge consists; and when a man once perceives how far they agree or disagree one with another, he will be able to judge of what other people say and will not need to be led by the arguments of others, which are many of them nothing but plausible sophistry. This will teach him to state the question right and see whereon it turns; and thus he will stand upon his own legs and know by his own understanding. Whereas by collecting and learning arguments by heart he will be but a retainer to others; and when anyone questions the foundations they are built upon, he will be at a nonplus and be fain to give up his implicit[46] knowledge.

16. *Haste*. Labour for labour sake is against nature. The understanding, as well as all the other faculties, chooses always the shortest way to its end, would presently obtain the knowledge it is about and then set upon some new enquiry. But this whether laziness or haste often misleads it and makes it content itself with improper ways of search and such as will not serve the turn. Sometimes

[44] See above, footnote 10.—F.W.G.

[45] That is, "relationships," "dispositions."—F.W.G.

[46] Compare section 24, p. 85 "second-hand or implicit knowledge"; that is, knowledge which cannot be made explicit because it is not his own but is taken on trust.—F.W.G.

it rests upon testimony, when testimony of right has nothing to do, because it is easier to believe than to be scientifically instructed. Sometimes it contents itself with one argument and rests satisfied with that, as it were a demonstration; whereas the thing under proof is not capable of demonstration and therefore must be submitted to the trial of probabilities, and all the material arguments pro and con be examined and brought to a balance. In some cases the mind is determined by probable topics in enquiries where demonstration may be had. All these and several others, which laziness, impatience, custom and want of use and attention lead men into, are misapplications of the understanding in the search of truth. In every question the nature and manner of the proof it is capable of should first be considered to make our enquiry such as it should be.[47] This would save a great deal of frequently misemployed pains and lead us sooner to that discovery and possession of truth we are capable of. The multiplying variety of arguments, especially frivolous ones, such as are all that are merely verbal, is not only lost labour, but cumbers the memory to no purpose and serves only to hinder it from seizing and holding of the truth in all those cases which are capable of demonstration. In such a way of proof the truth and certainty is seen and the mind fully possesses itself of it; when in the other way of assent it only hovers about it, is amused with uncertainties. In this superficial way indeed the mind is capable of more variety of plausible talk, but is not enlarged as it should be in its knowledge. It is to this same haste and impatience of the mind also that a not due tracing of the arguments to their

[47] An excellent piece of advice which is fully in accord with modern principles of methodology. Cf. section 36 on correct formulation of the problem.—F.W.G.

true foundation is owing; men see a little, presume a
great deal, and so jump to the conclusion. This is a short
way to fancy and conceit and (if firmly embraced) to
opiniatrety,[48] but is certainly the furthest way about
to knowledge. For he that will know must, by the connection of the proofs, see the truth and the ground it
stands on; and therefore, if he has for haste skipped over
what he should have examined, he must begin and go
over all again, or else he will never come to knowledge.

17. *Desultory*. Another fault of as ill consequence as
this, which proceeds also from laziness with a mixture of
vanity, is the skipping from one sort of knowledge to
another. Some men's tempers are quickly weary of any
one thing. Constancy and assiduity is what they cannot
bear; the same study long continued in is as intolerable
to them as the appearing long in the same clothes or
fashion is to a Court lady.

18. *Smattering*. Others, that they may seem universally knowing, get a little smattering in everything. Both
these may fill their heads with superficial notions of
things, but are very much out of the way of attaining
truth or knowledge.

19. *Universality*. I do not here speak against the taking
a taste of every sort of knowledge; it is certainly very
useful and necessary to form the mind, but then it must
be done in a different way and to a different end—not
for talk and vanity to fill the head with shreds of all
kinds, that he who is possessed of such a frippery may
be able to match the discourses of all he shall meet with,
as if nothing could come amiss to him and his head was
so well a stored magazine that nothing could be proposed
which he was not master of and was readily furnished to

---

[48] That is, "opinionatedness." "Opiniatrety" seems to be the correct form of the word; the text has "opiniatrity."—F.W.G.

entertain anyone on. This is an excellency indeed, and a great one too, to have a real and true knowledge in all or most of the objects of contemplation. But it is what the mind of one and the same man can hardly attain unto; and the instances are so few of those who have in any measure approached towards it, that I know not whether they are to be proposed as examples in the ordinary conduct of the understanding. For a man to understand fully the business of his particular calling in the commonwealth and of religion, which is his calling as he is a man in the world, is usually enough to take up his whole time; and there are few that inform themselves in these, which is every man's proper and peculiar business, so to the bottom as they should do. But though this be so, and there are very few men that extend their thoughts towards universal knowledge, yet I do not doubt but, if the right way were taken and the methods of enquiry were ordered as they should be, men of little business and great leisure might go a great deal further in it than is usually done. To return to the business in hand, the end and use of a little insight in those parts of knowledge which are not a man's proper business is to accustom our minds to all sorts of ideas and the proper ways of examining their habitudes and relations. This gives the mind a freedom, and the exercising the understanding in the several ways of enquiry and reasoning which the most skilful have made use of teaches the mind sagacity and wariness and a suppleness to apply itself more closely and dexterously to the bents and turns of the matter in all its researches. Besides, this universal taste of all the sciences with an indifferency, before the mind is possessed with any one in particular and grown into love and admiration of what is made its darling, will prevent another evil very com-

monly to be observed in those who have from the
beginning been seasoned only by one part of knowledge.
Let a man be given up to the contemplation of one sort
of knowledge, and that will become everything. The mind
will take such a tincture from a familiarity with that
object, that everything else, how remote soever, will be
brought under the same view. A metaphysician will
bring ploughing and gardening immediately to abstract
notions; the history of nature shall signify nothing to
him. An alchemist, on the contrary, shall reduce divinity to the maxims of his laboratory, explain morality by
sal, sulphur and mercury, and allegorise the Scripture
itself and the sacred mysteries thereof into the philosopher's stone.[49] And I heard once a man who had a
more than ordinary excellency in music seriously ac-
commodate Moses' seven days of the first week[50] to the
notes of music, as if from thence had been taken the
measure and method of the creation. It is of no small
consequence to keep the mind from such a possession,
which I think is best done by giving it a fair and equal
view of the whole intellectual world, wherein it may see
the order, rank and beauty of the whole, and give a just
allowance to the distinct provinces of the several sciences
in the due order and usefulness of each of them.

If this be that which old men will not think necessary
nor be easily brought to, it is fit at least that it should

[49] According to the sixteenth-century Swiss physician, Paracelsus,
salt, sulphur, and mercury were the main constituents of the human
body; sickness was due to their dissociation from one another or the
lack of balance between them. The "philosopher's stone" was supposed by mediaeval alchemists to be capable of transmuting base
metals into gold.—F.W.G.

[50] The reference is to the account of creation in Genesis 1 and 2.
The first five books of the Bible, the Pentateuch, were thought by
the Jews to be the work of Moses, and they were commonly re-
ferred to as "the books of Moses."—F.W.G.

be practised in the breeding of the young. The business of education, as I have already observed,[51] is not, as I think, to make them perfect in any one of the sciences, but so to open and dispose their minds as may best make them capable of any, when they shall apply themselves to it. If men are for a long time accustomed only to one sort or method of thoughts, their minds grow stiff in it and do not readily turn to another. It is therefore to give them this freedom that I think they should be made look into all sorts of knowledge and exercise their understandings in so wide a variety and stock of knowledge. But I do not propose it as a variety and stock of knowledge, but a variety and freedom of thinking, as an increase of the powers and activity of the mind, not as an enlargement of its possessions.

20. *Reading.* This is that which I think great readers are apt to be mistaken in. Those who have read of everything are thought to understand everything too; but it is not always so. Reading furnishes the mind only with materials of knowledge; it is thinking makes what we read ours. We are of the ruminating kind, and it is not enough to cram ourselves with a great load of collections; unless we chew them over again, they will not give us strength and nourishment. There are indeed in some writers visible instances of deep thought, close and acute reasoning and ideas well pursued. The light these would give would be of great use, if their readers would observe and imitate them; all the rest at best are but particulars fit to be turned into knowledge; but that can be done only by our own meditation and examining the reach, force and coherence of what is said; and then, as far as we apprehend and see the connection of ideas, so far it is ours; without that it is but so much loose

[51] Section 12.—F.W.G.

matter floating in our brain. The memory may be stored, but the judgement is little better and the stock of knowledge not increased by being able to repeat what others have said or produce the arguments we have found in them. Such a knowledge as this is but knowledge by hearsay, and the ostentation of it is at best but talking by rote, and very often upon weak and wrong principles. For all that is to be found in books is not built upon true foundations nor always rightly deduced from the principles it is pretended to be built on. Such an examen as is requisite to discover that, every reader's mind is not forward to make, especially in those who have given themselves up to a party and only hunt for what they can scrape together that may favour and support the tenets of it. Such men wilfully exclude themselves from truth and from all true benefit to be received by reading. Others of more indifferency often want attention and industry. The mind is backward in itself to be at the pains to trace every argument to its original and to see upon what basis it stands and how firmly; but yet it is this that gives so much the advantage to one man more than another in reading. The mind should by severe rules be tied down to this at first uneasy task; use and exercise will give it facility, so that those who are accustomed to it, readily, as it were with one cast of the eye, take a view of the argument and presently in most cases see where it bottoms. Those who have got this faculty, one may say, have got the true key of books and the clue to lead them through the mizmaze of variety of opinions and authors to truth and certainty. This young beginners should be entered in and showed the use of, that they might profit by their reading .Those who are strangers to it will be apt to think it too great a clog in the way of men's studies, and they will suspect they shall make but small progress if, in the books they read, they must stand to examine and unravel every argument and follow it step by step up to its original.

I answer, this is a good objection and ought to weigh with those whose reading is designed for much talk and little knowledge, and I have nothing to say to it. But I am here enquiring into the conduct of the understanding in its progress towards knowledge; and to those who aim at that I may say that he who fair and softly goes steadily forward in a course that points right will sooner be at his journey's end than he that runs after everyone he meets, though he gallop all day full speed.

To which let me add that this way of thinking on and profiting by what we read will be a clog and rub to anyone only in the beginning; when custom and exercise has made it familiar, it will be dispatched in most occasions without resting or interruption in the course of our reading. The motions and views of a mind exercised that way are wonderfully quick; and a man used to such sort of reflections sees as much at one glimpse as would require a long discourse to lay before another and make out in an entire and gradual deduction. Besides that, when the first difficulties are over, the delight and sensible advantage it brings mightily encourages and enlivens the mind in reading, which without this is very improperly called study.

21. *Intermediate principles.* As a help to this I think it may be proposed that, for the saving the long progression of the thoughts to remote and first principles in every case, the mind should provide itself several stages, that is to say, intermediate principles, which it might have recourse to in the examining those positions that come in its way. These, though they are not self-evident principles, yet, if they have been made out from them by

a wary and unquestionable deduction, may be depended on as certain and infallible truths and serve as unquestionable truths to prove other points depending on them by a nearer and shorter view than remote and general maxims. These may serve as landmarks to show what lies in the direct way of truth or is quite besides it. And thus mathematicians do, who do not in every new problem run it back to the first axioms through all the whole train of intermediate propositions. Certain theorems that they have settled to themselves upon sure demonstration serve to resolve to them multitudes of propositions which depend on them and are as firmly made out from thence as if the mind went afresh over every link of the whole chain that ties them to first self-evident principles. Only in other sciences great care is to be taken that they establish those intermediate principles with as much caution, exactness and indifferency as mathematicians use in the settling any of their great theorems. When this is not done, but men take up the principles in this or that science upon credit, inclination, interest, etc., in haste without due examination and most unquestionable proof, they lay a trap for themselves and as much as in them lies captivate their understandings to mistake, falsehood and error.

22. *Partiality*. As there is a partiality to opinions, which, as we have already observed, is apt to mislead the understanding, so there is often a partiality to studies, which is prejudicial also to knowledge and improvement. Those sciences which men are particularly versed in they are apt to value and extol, as if that part of knowledge which everyone has acquainted himself with were that alone which was worth the having, and all the rest were idle and empty amusements, comparatively of no use or importance. This is the effect of ignor-

ance and not knowledge, the being vainly puffed up
with a flatulency arising from a weak and narrow com-
prehension. It is not amiss that everyone should
relish the science that he has made his peculiar study;
a view of its beauties and a sense of its usefulness carries
a man on with the more delight and warmth in the
pursuit and improvement of it. But the contempt of all
other knowledge, as if it were nothing in comparison
of law or physic, of astronomy or chemistry, or perhaps
some yet meaner part of knowledge wherein I have got
some smattering or am somewhat advanced, is not only
the mark of a vain or little mind, but does this prejudice in the conduct of the understanding, that it coops it
up within narrow bounds and hinders it from looking
abroad into other provinces of the intellectual world,
more beautiful possibly and more fruitful than that
which it had till then laboured in; wherein it might
find, besides new knowledge, ways or hints whereby it
might be enabled the better to cultivate its own.

23. *Theology*. There is indeed one science (as they are
now distinguished) incomparably above all the rest, where
it is not by corruption narrowed into a trade or faction
for mean or ill ends and secular interests; I mean theology, which, containing the knowledge of God and his
creatures, our duty to him and our fellow creatures and a
view of our present and future state, is the comprehen-
sion of all other knowledge directed to its true end,
i.e., the honour and veneration of the Creator and the
happiness of mankind. This is that noble study which is
every man's duty and everyone that can be called a rational creature is capable of. The works of nature and
the words of revelation display it to mankind in characters so large and visible, that those who are not
quite blind may in them read and see the first princi-

ples and most necessary parts of it and from thence, as
they have time and industry, may be enabled to go on to
the more abstruse parts of it and penetrate into those
infinite depths filled with the treasures of wisdom and
knowledge. This is that science which would truly enlarge men's minds, were it studied or permitted to be
studied everywhere with that freedom, love of truth
and charity which it teaches, and were not made, contrary to its nature, the occasion of strife, faction, ma-
lignity and narrow impositions. I shall say no more here
of this, but that it is undoubtedly a wrong use of my
understanding to make it the rule and measure of another man's, a use which it is neither fit for nor capable of.

24. *Partiality.* This partiality, where it is not permitted an authority to render all other studies insignificant
or contemptible, is often indulged so far as to be relied
upon and made use of in other parts of knowledge to
which it does not at all belong and wherewith it has no
manner of affinity. Some men have so used their heads
to mathematical figures that, giving a preference to the
methods of that science, they introduce lines and dia-
grams into their studies of divinity or politic[al] enquiries, as if nothing could be known without them; and
others, accustomed to retired speculations, run natural
philosophy into metaphysical notions and the abstract
generalities of logic; and how often may one meet with
religion and morality treated of in the terms of the laboratory and thought to be improved by the methods and
notations of chemistry. But he that will take care of the
conduct of his understanding to direct it right to the
knowledge of things must avoid those undue mixtures
and not, by a fondness for what he has found useful
and necessary in one, transfer it to another science where

it serves only to perplex and confound the understanding. It is a certain truth that *res nolunt male administrari;*[52] it is no less certain *res nolunt male intelligi.*[53] Things themselves are to be considered as they are in themselves, and then they will show us in what way they are to be understood. For to have right conceptions about them we must bring our understandings to the inflexible natures and unalterable relations of things, and not endeavour to bring things to any preconceived notions of our own.[54]

There is another partiality very commonly observable in men of study, no less prejudicial nor ridiculous than the former, and that is a fantastical and wild attributing all knowledge to the ancients alone or to the moderns. This raving upon antiquity in matter of poetry Horace has wittily described and exposed in one of his satires.[55] The same sort of madness may be found in reference to all the other sciences. Some will not admit an opinion not authorised by men of old, who were then all giants in knowledge; nothing is to be put into the treasury of truth or knowledge which has not the stamp of Greece or Rome upon it; and since their days will scarce allow that men have been able to see, think or write. Others, with a like extravagancy, contemn all that the ancients have left us and, being taken with the modern inventions and discoveries, lay by all that went before, as if whatever is called old must have the decay of time upon it and truth too were liable to mould and rottenness.

[52] "Things are unwilling (do not allow themselves) to be badly handled."—F.W.G.

[53] "Things are unwilling (do not allow themselves) to be wrongly understood."—F.W.G.

[54] The last sentences of this paragraph are an emphatic assertion of Locke's empirical position.—F.W.G.

[55] Actually in his *Epistles,* II, i.—F.W.G.

Men, I think, have been much the same for natural endowments in all times. Fashion, discipline and education have put eminent differences in the ages of several countries and made one generation much differ from another in arts and sciences; but truth is always the same; time alters it not, nor is it the better or worse for being of ancient or modern tradition. Many were eminent in former ages of the world for their discovery and delivery of it; but though the knowledge they have left us be worth our study, yet they exhausted not all its treasure; they left a great deal for the industry and sagacity of after ages, and so shall we. That was once new to them which anyone now receives with veneration for its antiquity; nor was it the worse for appearing as a novelty, and that which is now embraced for its newness will, to posterity, be old but not thereby be less true or less genuine. There is no occasion on this account to oppose the ancients and the moderns to one another or to be squeamish on either side. He that wisely conducts his mind in the pursuit of knowledge will gather what lights and get what helps he can from either of them, from whom they are best to be had, without adoring the errors or rejecting the truths which he may find mingled in them.

Another partiality may be observed, in some to vulgar, in others to heterodox tenets. Some are apt to conclude that what is the common opinion cannot but be true; so many men's eyes, they think, cannot but see right; so many men's understandings of all sorts cannot be deceived; and therefore [they] will not venture to look beyond the received notions of the place and age nor have so presumptuous a thought as to be wiser than their neighbours. They are content to go with the crowd, and so go easily, which they think is going right or at least serves them as well. But however *vox populi vox Dei*[56] has prevailed as a maxim, yet I do not remember wherever God delivered his oracles by the multitude or nature truths by the herd. On the other side, some fly all common opinions as either false or frivolous. The title of many-headed beast[57] is a sufficient reason to them to conclude that no truths of weight or consequence can be lodged there. Vulgar opinions are suited to vulgar capacities and adapted to the ends of those that govern. He that will know the truth of things must leave the common and beaten tract, which none but weak and servile minds are satisfied to trudge along continually in. Such nice[58] palates relish nothing but strange notions quite out of the way; whatever is commonly received has the mark of the beast[59] on it, and they think it a lessening to them to harken to it or receive it; their mind runs only after paradoxes; these they seek, these they embrace, these alone they vent, and so, as they think, distinguish themselves from the vulgar. But common or uncommon are not the marks to distinguish truth or falsehood and therefore should not be any bias to us in our enquiries. We should not judge of things by men's opinions, but of opinions by things. The multitude reason but ill, and therefore may be well suspected and cannot be relied on nor should be followed as a sure guide; but philosophers who have quitted the orthodoxy of the

[56] "The voice of the people is the voice of God." The Latin words occur in a letter from the eighth century scholar Alcuin to the Emperor Charlemagne.—F.W.G.

[57] Compare Shakespeare, *Coriolanus,* IV, i, 1: "The beast with many heads butts me away"; and Massinger, *The Unnatural Combat,* III, ii: "Fury of the many-headed monster, the giddy multitude."—F.W.G.

[58] That is, "finicky."—F.W.G.

[59] Compare Rev. 13:17: "The mark, even the name, of the beast." —F.W.G.

community and the popular doctrines of their countries have fallen into as extravagant and as absurd opinions as ever common reception countenanced. It would be madness to refuse to breathe the common air or quench one's thirst with water because the rabble use them to these purposes; and if there are conveniences of life which common use reaches not, it is not reason to reject them because they are not grown into the ordinary fashion of the country and every villager does not know them.

Truth, whether in or out of fashion, is the measure of knowledge and the business of the understanding; whatsoever is besides that, however authorised by consent or recommended by rarity, is nothing but ignorance or something worse.

Another sort of partiality there is whereby men impose upon themselves and by it make their reading little useful to themselves; I mean the making use of the opinions of writers and laying stress upon their authorities wherever they find them to favour their own opinions.

There is nothing almost has done more harm to men dedicated to letters than giving the name of study to reading and making a man of great reading to be the same with a man of great knowledge, or at least to be a title of honour. All that can be recorded in writing are only facts or reasonings. Facts are of three sorts:

1. Merely of natural agents, observable in the ordinary operations of bodies one upon another, whether in the visible course of things left to themselves, or in experiments made by men applying agents and patients[60]

---

[60] For instance, in chemical experiments where two substances are brought together in order to observe the reaction between them. "Patient" here means the recipient of an activity, that which undergoes it.—F.W.G.

to one another after a peculiar and artificial manner.

2. Of voluntary agents, more especially the actions of men in society, which makes civil and moral history.

3. Of opinions.[61]

In these three consists, as it seems to me, that which commonly has the name of learning; to which perhaps some may add a distinct head of critical writings, which indeed at bottom is nothing but matter of fact and resolves itself into this, that such a man or set of men used such a word or phrase in such a sense, i.e. that they made such sounds the marks of such ideas.[62]

Under reasonings I comprehend all the discoveries of general truths made by human reason, whether found by intuition, demonstration or probable deductions.[63] And this is that which is, if not alone knowledge (because the truth or probability of particular propositions may be known too), yet is, as may be supposed, most properly the business of those who pretend to improve their understandings and make themselves knowing by reading.

Books and reading are looked upon to be the great helps of the understanding and instruments of knowledge, as it must be allowed that they are; and yet I beg leave to question whether these do not prove a hindrance to many and keep several bookish men from attaining to solid and true knowledge. This, I think, I may be permitted to say, that there is no part wherein the understanding needs a more careful and wary conduct

[61] Locke is not suggesting that facts and opinions are identical, but that opinions can be observed and recorded as fact.—F.W.G.

[62] Here and in the sentence above, "All that can be recorded in writing are only facts or reasonings," Locke seems to disregard the aesthetic potentiality of language. See *Thoughts*, § 174, on poetry. —F.W.G.

[63] See Introduction, p. 19.

than in the use of books; without which they will prove
rather innocent amusements than profitable employ-
ments of our time, and bring but small additions to our
knowledge.

There is not seldom to be found, even amongst those
who aim at knowledge, [those] who with an unwearied
industry employ their whole time in books, who scarce
allow themselves time to eat or sleep, but read and read
and read on, but yet make no great advances in real
knowledge, though there be no defect in their intellectual faculties, to which their little progress can be im-
puted. The mistake here is, that it is usually supposed
that, by reading, the author's knowledge is transfused
into the reader's understanding; and so it is, but not by
bare reading, but by reading and understanding what he
writ. Whereby I mean, not barely comprehending what
is affirmed or denied in each proposition (though that
great readers do not always think themselves concerned
precisely to do), but to see and follow the train of his
reasonings, observe the strength and clearness of their
connection and examine upon what they bottom. Without this a man may read the discourses of a very rational
author, writ in a language and in propositions that he
very well understands, and yet acquire not one jot of his
knowledge; which consisting only in the perceived, certain or probable connection of the ideas made use of in
his reasonings, the reader's knowledge is no further increased than he perceives that, so much as he sees of this
connection, so much he knows of the truth or probability
of that author's opinions.

All that he relies on without this perception he takes
upon trust upon the author's credit without any knowledge of it at all. This makes me not at all wonder to see
some men so abound in citations and build so much

upon authorities, it being the sole foundation on which
they bottom most of their own tenets; so that in effect
they have but a second hand or implicit knowledge,[64] i.e.
are in the right if such an one from whom they borrowed
it were in the right in that opinion which they took
from him, which indeed is no knowledge at all. Writers
of this or former ages may be good witnesses of matters
of fact which they deliver, which we may do well to take
upon their authority; but their credit can go no further
than this; it cannot at all affect the truth and falsehood
of opinions, which have another sort of trial by reason
and proof, which they themselves made use of to make
themselves knowing, and so must others too that will
partake in their knowledge. Indeed it is an advantage
that they have been at the pains to find out the proofs
and lay them in that order that may show the truth or
probability of their conclusions; and for this we owe
them great acknowledgements for saving us the pains in
searching out those proofs which they have collected for
us and which possibly, after all our pains, we might not
have found nor been able to set them in so good a light
as that which they left them us in. Upon this account we
are mightily beholding to judicious writers of all ages
for those discoveries and discourses they have left be-
hind them for our instruction, if we know how to make a
right use of them; which is not to run them over in a
hasty perusal and perhaps lodge their opinions or some
remarkable passages in our memories, but to enter into
their reasonings, examine their proofs, and then judge of
the truth or falsehood, probability or improbability of
what they advance, not by any opinion we have entertained of the author, but by the evidence he produces
and the conviction he affords us drawn from things

[64] See footnote 46.—F.W.G.

themselves. Knowing is seeing, and, if it be so, it is madness to persuade ourselves that we do so by another
man's eyes, let him use never so many words to tell us
that what he asserts is very visible. Till we ourselves see
it with our own eyes and perceive it by our own understandings, we are as much in the dark and as void of
knowledge as before, let us believe any learned author
as much as we will.

Euclid and Archimedes are allowed to be knowing
and to have demonstrated what they say; and yet whoso-
ever shall read over their writings without perceiving the
connection of their proofs and seeing what they shew,
though he may understand all their words, yet he is not
the more knowing; he may believe indeed but does not
know what they say, and so is not advanced one jot in
mathematical knowledge by all his reading of those ap-
proved mathematicians.

25. *Haste.* The eagerness and strong bent of the mind
after knowledge, if not warily regulated, is often a hindrance to it. It still presses into further discoveries and
new objects and catches at the variety of knowledge, and
therefore often stays not long enough on what is before
it to look into it as it should, for haste to pursue what is
yet out of sight. He that rides post through a country
may be able from the transient view to tell how in general the parts lie, and may be able to give some loose
description of here a mountain and there a plain, here a
morass and there a river, woodland in one part and
savannas in another. Such superficial ideas and observations as these he may collect in galloping over it. But the
more useful observations of the soil, plants, animals and
inhabitants with their several sorts and properties must
necessarily escape him; and it is seldom men ever discover the rich mines without some digging. Nature com-

monly lodges her treasure and jewels in rocky ground. If the matter be knotty and the sense lies deep, the mind must stop and buckle to it and stick upon it with labour and thought and close contemplation, and not leave it till it has mastered the difficulty and got possession of truth. But here care must be taken to avoid the other extreme: a man must not stick at every useless nicety and expect mysteries of science in every trivial question or scruple that he may raise. He that will stand to pick up and examine every pebble that comes in his way is as unlikely to return enriched and loaded with jewels as the other that travelled full speed. Truths are not the better nor the worse for their obviousness or difficulty, but their value is to be measured by their usefulness and tendency.[65] Insignificant[66] observations should not take up any of our minutes, and those that enlarge our view and give light towards further and useful discoveries should not be neglected, though they stop our course and spend some of our time in a fixed attention.

There is another haste that does often and will mislead the mind, if it be left to itself and its own conduct. The understanding is naturally forward, not only to learn its knowledge by variety (which makes it skip over one to get speedily to another part of knowledge), but also eager to enlarge its views by running too fast into general observations and conclusions without a due examination of particulars enough whereon to found those general axioms. This seems to enlarge their stock, but it is of fancies not realities; such theories built upon narrow foundations stand but weakly, and, if they fall not of themselves, are at least very hardly to be supported

[65] Locke regularly makes utility a criterion of value; see also *Thoughts,* §§ 197, 201 ff.—F.W.G.

[66] That is, "meaningless."—F.W.G.

against the assaults of opposition. And thus men, being too hasty to erect to themselves general notions and ill-grounded theories, find themselves deceived in their stock of knowledge when they come to examine their hastily assumed maxims themselves or to have them attacked by others. General observations drawn from particulars are the jewels of knowledge, comprehending great store in a little room; but they are therefore to be made with the greater care and caution, lest, if we take counterfeit for true, our loss and shame be the greater when our stock comes to a severe scrutiny. One or two particulars may suggest hints of enquiry, and they do well who take those hints; but if they turn them into conclusions and make them presently general rules, they are forward indeed, but it is only to impose on themselves by propositions assumed for truths without sufficient warrant. To make such observations is, as has been already remarked,[67] to make the head a magazine of materials which can hardly be called knowledge, or at least it is but like a collection of lumber not reduced to use or order; and he that makes everything an observation has the same useless plenty and much more falsehood mixed with it. The extremes on both sides are to be avoided, and he will be able to give the best account of his studies who keeps his understanding in the right mean between them.

26. *Anticipation*. Whether it be a love of that which brings the first light and information to their minds and want of vigour and industry to enquire, or else that men content themselves with any appearance of knowledge, right or wrong, which when they have once got they will hold fast, this is visible, that many men give themselves up to the first anticipations of their minds and are very

[67] Sections 13 and 20.—F.W.G.

tenacious of the opinions that first possess them. They are often as fond of their first conceptions as of their first born, and will by no means recede from the judgement they have once made or any conjecture or conceit which they have once entertained. This is a fault in the conduct of the understanding, since this firmness or rather stiffness of the mind is not from an adherence to truth but a submission to prejudice. It is an unreasonable homage paid to prepossession, whereby we show a reverence not to (what we pretend to seek) truth, but what by haphazard we chance to light on, be it what it will. This is visibly a preposterous use of our faculties and is a downright prostituting of the mind to resign it thus and put it under the power of the first comer. This can never be allowed or ought to be followed as a right way to knowledge, till the understanding (whose business it is to conform itself to what it finds on the objects without) can by its own opiniatrety change that and make the unalterable nature of things comply with its own hasty determinations, which will never be. Whatever we fancy, things keep their course, and their habitudes, correspondences and relations keep the same to one another.

27. *Resignation*. Contrary to these, but by a like dangerous excess on the other side, are those who always resign their judgement to the last man they heard or read. Truth never sinks into these men's minds nor gives any tincture to them, but, chameleon-like, they take the colour of what is laid before them and as soon lose and resign it to the next that happens to come in their way. The order wherein opinions are proposed or received by us is no rule of their rectitude nor ought to be a cause of their preference. First or last in this case is the effect of chance and not the measure of truth or falsehood. This

everyone must confess and therefore should in the pursuit of truth keep his mind free from the influence of any such accidents. A man may as reasonably draw cuts for his tenets, regulate his persuasion by the cast of a die, as take it up for its novelty or retain it because it had his first assent and he was never of another mind. Well-weighed reasons are to determine the judgement; those the mind should be always ready to harken and submit to and by their testimony and suffrage entertain or reject any tenet indifferently, whether it be a perfect stranger or an old acquaintance.

28. *Practice*. Though the faculties of the mind are improved by exercise, yet they must not be put to a stress beyond their strength. *Quid valeant humeri, quid ferre recusent*[68] must be made the measure of everyone's understanding who has a desire not only to perform well but to keep up the vigour of his faculties and not to baulk his understanding by what is too hard for it. The mind, by being engaged in a task beyond its strength, like the body strained by lifting at a weight too heavy, has often its force broken and thereby gets an unaptness or an aversion to any vigorous attempt ever after. A sinew cracked seldom recovers its former strength, or at least the tenderness of the sprain remains a good while after and the memory of it longer, and leaves a lasting caution in the man not to put the part quickly again to any robust employment. So it fares in the mind once jaded by an attempt above its power; it either is disabled for the future or else checks at any vigorous undertaking ever after, at least is very hardly brought to exert its

---

[68] Horace, *Ars Poetica*, ll. 39–40:
> *Et versate diu quid ferre recusent,*
>   *Quid valeant humeri.*

"Consider for a long time what the shoulders refuse to bear and what they have the strength for."—F.W.G.

force again on any subject that requires thought and meditation. The understanding should be brought to the difficult and knotty parts of knowledge, that try the strength of thought, and a full bent of the mind by insensible degrees;[69] and in such a gradual proceeding nothing is too hard for it. Nor let it be objected that such a slow progress will never reach the extent of some sciences. It is not to be imagined how far constancy will carry a man; however, it is better walking slowly in a rugged way than to break a leg and be a cripple. He that begins with the calf may carry the ox; but he that will at first go to take up an ox may so disable himself as not be able to lift a calf after that. When the mind by insensible degrees has brought itself to attention and close thinking, it will be able to cope with difficulties and master them without any prejudice to itself, and then it may go on roundly. Every abstruse problem, every intricate question will not baffle, discourage or break it. But though putting the mind unprepared upon an unusual stress that may discourage or damp it for the future ought to be avoided, yet this must not run it, by an over great shyness of difficulties, into a lazy sauntering about ordinary and obvious things that demand no thought or application. This debases and enervates the understanding, makes it weak and unfit for labour. This is a sort of hovering about the surface of things without any insight into them or penetration; and when the mind has been once habituated to this lazy recumbency and satisfaction on the obvious surface of things, it is in danger to rest satisfied there and go no deeper, since it

[69] This is the punctuation of the text; it requires that "to" be understood before "a full bent." The editions of Fowler and Adamson have: "The understanding should be brought to the difficult and knotty parts of knowledge, that try the strength of thought and a full bent of the mind, by insensible degrees."—F.W.G.

cannot do it without pains and digging. He that has for some time accustomed himself to take up with what easily offers itself at first view, has reason to fear he shall never reconcile himself to the fatigue of turning and tumbling things in his mind to discover their more retired and more valuable secrets.

It is not strange that methods of learning which scholars have been accustomed to in their beginning and entrance upon the sciences should influence them all their lives and be settled in their minds by an over-ruling reverence, especially if they be such as universal use has established. Learners must at first be believers, and, their master's rules having once been made axioms to them, it is no wonder they should keep that dignity[70] and by the authority they have once got mislead those who think it sufficient to excuse them if they go out of their way in a well beaten tract.

29. *Words.* I have copiously enough spoken of the abuse of words in another place[71] and therefore shall upon this reflection, that the sciences are full of them, warn those that would conduct their understandings right not to take any term, howsoever authorised by the language of the schools, to stand for any thing till they have an idea of it. A word may be of frequent use and great credit with several authors and be by them made use of as if it stood for some real being; but yet, if he that reads cannot frame any distinct idea of that being, it is certain[ly] to him a mere empty sound without a meaning, and he learns no more by all that is said of it or attributed to it than if it were affirmed only of that

[70] There appears to be some play on words here; *dignitas* is the Latin equivalent of the Greek *axioma,* and "dignity" could be regarded as a synonym for axiom—it was so used by Sir Thomas Browne.—F.W.G.

[71] *Essay,* III, especially x.

bare empty sound. They who would advance in knowledge and not deceive and swell themselves with a little articulated air should lay down this as a fundamental rule, not to take words for things nor suppose that names in books signify real entities in nature till they can frame clear and distinct ideas of those entities. It will not perhaps be allowed if I should set down "substantial forms" and "intentional species"[72] as such that may justly be suspected to be of this kind of insignificant terms. But this I am sure, to one that can form no determined ideas of what they stand for they signify nothing at all; and all that he thinks he knows about them is to him so much knowledge about nothing and amounts at most but to a learned ignorance. It is not without all reason supposed that there are many such empty terms to be found in some learned writers, to which they had recourse to etch[73] out their systems where their understandings could not furnish them with conceptions from things. But yet I believe the supposing of some realities in nature answering those and the like words have much perplexed some and quite misled others in the study of nature. That which in any discourse signifies "I know not what"[74] should be considered "I know not when." Where men have any conceptions, they can, if they are never so abstruse or abstracted, explain them and the terms they use for them. For our conceptions being nothing but ideas, which are all made up of simple ones,[75] if they cannot give us the ideas their words stand for, it is plain they have none. To what purpose can it be to hunt after his conceptions who has none or none

[72] Phrases used by the followers of the Peripatetic or Aristotelian philosophy.—F.W.G.

[73] That is, "eke."—F.W.G.

[74] See *Essay*, II, xxiii, 2.

[75] On simple and complex ideas, see *Essay*, II, ii and xii.—F.W.G.

distinct? He that knew not what he himself meant by a
learned term cannot make us know anything by his use
of it, let us beat our heads about it never so long.
Whether we are able to comprehend all the operations
of nature and the manners of them, it matters not to
enquire; but this is certain, that we can comprehend no
more of them than we can distinctly conceive; and therefore to obtrude terms where we have no distinct conceptions, as if they did contain or rather conceal something,
is but an artifice of learned vanity to cover a defect in
a hypothesis or our understandings. Words are not
made to conceal, but to declare and show something;
where they are, by those who pretend to instruct, otherwise used, they conceal indeed something; but that that
they conceal is nothing but the ignorance, error or sophistry of the talker, for there is, in truth, nothing else
under them.

30. *Wandering.* That there is constant succession and
flux of ideas in our minds I have observed in the former
part of this essay,[76] and everyone may take notice of it in
himself. This I suppose may deserve some part of our
care in the conduct of our understandings; and I think it
may be of great advantage if we can by use get that
power over our minds as to be able to direct that train
of ideas, that so, since there will new ones perpetually
come into our thoughts by a constant succession, we may
be able by choice so to direct them, that none may come
into view but such as are pertinent to our present enquiry, and in such order as may be most useful to the
discovery we are upon; or at least, if some foreign and
unsought ideas will offer themselves, that yet we might

---

[76] That is, the *Essay Concerning Human Understanding,* of which
Conduct was intended to be the last part; especially Book II.—
F.W.G.

be able to reject them and keep them from taking off our minds from its present pursuit and hinder them from running away with our thoughts quite from the subject in hand. This is not, I suspect, so easy to be done as perhaps may be imagined; and yet, for ought I know, this may be, if not the chief, yet one of the great differences that carry some men in their reasoning so far beyond others, where they seem to be naturally of equal parts. A proper and effectual remedy for this wandering of thoughts I would be glad to find. He that shall propose such a one would do great service to the studious and contemplative part of mankind and perhaps help unthinking men to become thinking. I must acknowledge that hitherto I have discovered no other way to keep our thoughts close to their business but the endeavouring as much as we can and by frequent attention and application getting the habit of attention and application. He that will observe children will find that, even when they endeavour their uttermost, they cannot keep their minds from straggling. The way to cure it, I am satisfied, is not angry chiding or beating,[77] for that presently fills their heads with all the ideas that fear, dread, or confusion can offer to them. To bring back gently their wandering thoughts by leading them into the path and going before them in the train they should pursue, without any rebuke or so much as taking notice (where it can be avoided) of their roving, I suppose would sooner reconcile and inure them to attention than all those rougher methods which more distract their thought and, hindering the application they would promote, introduce a contrary habit.

31. *Distinction.* Distinction and division[78] are (if I

[77] Compare *Thoughts,* § 77 etc.
[78] In the logical vocabulary of Locke's time "distinction" was the

mistake not the import of the words) very different
things, the one being the perception of a difference that
nature has placed in things, the other our making a division where there is yet none. At least, if I may be permitted to consider them in this sense, I think I may say
of them that one of them is the most necessary and con-
ducive to true knowledge that can be, the other, when
too much made use of, serves only to puzzle and confound the understanding. To observe every the least difference that is in things argues a quick and clear sight,
and this keeps the understanding steady and right in its
way to knowledge. But though it be useful to discern
every variety [that] is to be found in nature, yet it is not
convenient[79] to consider every difference that is in things
and divide them into distinct classes under every such
difference. This will run us, if followed, into particulars
(for every individual has something that differences it
from another), and we shall be able to establish no general truths, or else at least shall be apt to perplex the
mind about them. The collection of several things into
several classes gives the mind more general and larger
views; but we must take care to unite them only in that
and so far as they do agree, for so far they may be united
under the consideration. For entity[80] itself that compre-

---

determining of different meanings in an ambiguous term or sentence; "division" was the determining of different species within the
same genus. The former was used more especially in the sphere of
language, the latter in that of natural objects. Locke does not make
his meaning entirely clear, but he is evidently cautioning his readers against excessive nicety in (verbal) distinction and commending
the precise observation of natural differences in things, though even
the latter, he points out, can be taken too far, so that it "will run
us, if followed, into particulars. . . ." Here, as so often, he has in
mind the hair-splitting arguments of contemporary disputation.—
F.W.G.

[79] That is, "fitting."—F.W.G.

[80] That is, "being."—F.W.G.

hends all things, as general as it is, may afford us clear
and rational conceptions. If we would well weigh and
keep in our minds what it is we are considering, that
would best instruct us when we should or should not
branch into further distinctions, which are to be taken
only from a due contemplation of things; to which there
is nothing more opposite than the art of verbal distinctions, made at pleasure in learned and arbitrarily in-
vented terms, to be applied at a venture without comprehending or conveying any distinct notions, and so
altogether fitted to artificial talk or empty noise in dispute without any clearing of difficulties or advance in
knowledge. Whatsoever subject we examine and would
get knowledge in we should, I think, make as general
and as large as it will bear; nor can there be any danger
of this if the idea of it be settled and determined;[81] for if
that be so, we shall easily distinguish it from any other
idea, though comprehended under the same name. For
it is to fence against the entanglements of equivocal
words and the great art of sophistry which lies in them
that distinctions have been multiplied and their use
thought so necessary. But had every distinct abstract
idea a distinct known name, there would be little need
of these multiplied scholastic distinctions, though there
would be nevertheless as much need still of the mind's
observing the differences that are in things and discrim-
inating them thereby one from another. It is not therefore the right way to knowledge to hunt after and fill the
head with abundance of artificial and scholastic distinctions, wherewith learned men's writings are often filled;
and we sometimes find what they treat of so divided and
subdivided that the mind of the most attentive reader
loses the sight of it, as it is more than probable the writer

[81] See footnote 10.—F.W.G.

himself did; for in things crumbled into dust it is in
vain to affect or pretend order or expect clearness. To
avoid confusion by too few or too many divisions is a
great skill in thinking as well as writing, which is but
the copying our thoughts; but what are the boundaries
of the mean between the two vicious excesses on both
hands, I think is hard to set down in words; clear and
distinct ideas[82] is all that I yet know able to regulate it.
But as to verbal distinctions received and applied to
common terms, i.e. equivocal words, they are more properly, I think, the business of criticisms and dictionaries
than of real knowledge and philosophy, since they for
the most part explain the meaning of words and give us
their several significations. The dexterous management
of terms and being able to "fend" and "prove"[83] with
them I know has and does pass in the world for a great
part of learning; but it is learning distinct from knowledge, for knowledge consists only in perceiving the habitudes and relations of ideas one to another, which is
done without words; the intervention of a sound helps
nothing to it. And hence we see that there is least use of
distinctions where there is most knowledge; I mean in
mathematics, where men have determined ideas with
known names to them; and so, there being no room for
equivocations, there is no need of distinctions. In arguing, the opponent uses as comprehensive and equivocal
terms as he can, to involve his adversary in the doubtful-
ness of his expressions; this is expected, and therefore
the answerer on his side makes it his play to distinguish
as much as he can and thinks he can never do it too
much; nor can he indeed in that way wherein victory
may be had without truth and without knowledge. This

[82] See footnote 10.—F.W.G.
[83] Terms used in disputation: "fend" means "argue."—F.W.G.

seems to me to be the art of disputing. Use your words as captiously as you can in your arguing on one side, and apply distinctions as much as you can on the other side to every term to nonplus your opponent; so that in this sort of scholarship, there being no bounds set to distinguishing, some men have thought all acuteness to have lain in it; and therefore in all they have read or thought on, their great business has been to amuse themselves with distinctions and multiply to themselves divisions, at least, more than the nature of the thing required. There seems to me, as I said, to be no other rule for this but a due and right consideration of things as they are in themselves. He that has settled in his mind determined ideas with names affixed to them will be able both to discern their differences one from another (which is really distinguishing) and, where the penury of words affords not terms answering every distinct idea, will be able to apply proper distinguishing terms to the comprehensive and equivocal names he is forced to make use of. This is all the need I know of distinguishing terms; and in such verbal distinctions each term of the distinction, joined to that whose signification it distinguishes, is but a new distinct name for a distinct idea. Where they are so and men have clear and distinct conceptions that answer their verbal distinctions, they are right, and are pertinent as far as they serve to clear anything in the subject under consideration. And this is that which seems to me the proper and only measure of distinctions and divisions; which he that will conduct his understanding right must not look for in the acuteness of invention nor the authority of writers, but will find only in the consideration of things themselves, whether they are led into it by their own meditations or the information of books.

An aptness to jumble things together wherein can be
found any likeness is a fault in the understanding on the
other side which will not fail to mislead it and, by thus
lumping of things, hinder the mind from distinct and
accurate conceptions of them.

32. *Similes.* To which let me here add another near of
kin to this, at least in name, and that is letting the mind
upon the suggestion of any new notion run immediately
after similes to make it the clearer to itself; which,
though it may be a good way and useful in the explain-
ing our thoughts to others, yet it is by no means a right
method to settle true notions of anything in ourselves,
because similes always fail in some part and come short
of that exactness which our conceptions should have to
things, if we would think aright.[84] This indeed makes
men plausible talkers; for those are always most accept-
able in discourse who have the way to let in their
thoughts into other men's minds with the greatest ease
and facility; whether those thoughts are well formed and
correspond with things matters not; few men care to be
instructed but at an easy rate. They who in their discourse strike the fancy and take the hearers' conceptions
along with them as fast as their words flow, are the applauded talkers and go for the only men of clear thoughts.
Nothing contributes so much to this as similes, whereby
men think they themselves understand better because they
are the better understood. But it is one thing to think
right and another thing to know the right way to lay our
thoughts before others with advantage and clearness, be
they right or wrong. Well chosen similes, metaphors and

[84] Despite what he says here, Locke regularly, and often delightfully, uses imagery in his writing; however, he was evidently aware
of its dangers and would no doubt excuse himself on the grounds
that his "borrowed and allusive ideas" do in fact follow "real and
solid truth."—F.W.G.

allegories, with method and order, do this the best of anything, because, being taken from objects already known and familiar to the understanding, they are conceived as fast as spoken; and the correspondence being concluded, the thing they are brought to explain and elucidate is thought to be understood too. Thus fancy passes for knowledge, and what is prettily said is mistaken for solid. I say not this to decry metaphor, or with design to take away that ornament of speech; my business here is not with rhetoricians and orators, but with philosophers and lovers of truth; to whom I would beg leave to give this one rule whereby to try whether, in the application of their thoughts to anything for the improvement of their knowledge, they do in truth comprehend the matter before them really such as it is in itself. The way to discover this is to observe whether, in the laying it before themselves or others, they make use only of borrowed representations and ideas foreign to the thing, which are applied to it by way of accommodation, as bearing some proportion or imagined likeness to the subject under consideration. Figured and metaphorical expressions do well to illustrate more abstruse and unfamiliar ideas which the mind is not yet thoroughly accustomed to; but then they must be made use of to illustrate ideas that we already have, not to paint to us those which we yet have not. Such borrowed and allusive ideas may follow real and solid truth, to set it off when found, but must by no means be set in its place and taken for it. If all our search has yet reached no further than simile and metaphor, we may assure ourselves we rather fancy than know and are not yet penetrated into the inside and reality of the thing, be it what it will, but content ourselves with what our imaginations, not things themselves, furnish us with.

33. *Assent.*[85] In the whole conduct of the understanding there is nothing of more moment than to know when and where and how far to give assent, and possibly there is nothing harder. It is very easily said, and nobody questions it, that giving and witholding our assent, and the degrees of it, should be regulated by the evidence which things carry with them; and yet we see men are not the better for this rule; some firmly embrace doctrines upon slight grounds, some upon no grounds, and some contrary to appearance. Some admit of certainty and are not to be moved in what they hold; others waver in everything, and there want not those that reject all as uncertain. What then shall a novice, an enquirer, a stranger do in the case? I answer, use his eyes. There is a correspondence in things, and agreement and disagreement in ideas, discernible in very different degrees, and there are eyes in men to see them if they please, only their eyes may be dimmed or dazzled and the discerning sight in them impaired or lost. Interest and passion dazzle; the custom of arguing on any side even against our persuasions, dims the understanding and makes it by degrees lose the faculty of discerning clearly between truth and falsehood, and so of adhering to the right side. It is not safe to play with error and dress it up to ourselves or others in the shape of truth. The mind by degrees loses its natural relish of real solid truth, is reconciled insensibly to anything that can but be dressed up into any faint[86] appearance of it; and if the fancy be allowed the place of judgement at first in sport, it afterwards comes by use to usurp it, and what is recommended by this flatterer (that studies but to please) is received for

85 See *Essay,* IV, xvi.
86 The text and Fowler, *op. cit.,* use "faint"; but Adamson, *op. cit.,* has "feint," the past participle of "feign."—F.W.G.

good. There are so many ways of fallacy, such arts of giving colours, appearances and resemblances by this court-dresser, the fancy, that he who is not wary to admit nothing but truth itself, very careful not to make his mind subservient to anything else, cannot but be caught. He that has a mind to believe has half assented already; and he that by often arguing against his own sense imposes falsehoods on others is not far from believing himself. This takes away the great distance there is betwixt truth and falsehood; it brings them almost together and makes it no great odds, in things that approach so near, which you take; and when things are brought to that pass, passion or interest, etc., easily and without being perceived determine which shall be the right.

34. *Indifferency.*[87] I have said above that we should keep a perfect indifferency for all opinions, not wish any of them true or try to make them appear so, but, being indifferent, receive and embrace them according as evidence and that alone gives the attestation of truth. They that do thus, i.e. keep their minds indifferent to opinions, to be determined only by evidence, will always find the understanding has perception enough to distinguish between evidence or no evidence, betwixt plain and doubtful; and if they neither give nor refuse their assent but by that measure, they will be safe in the opinions they have. Which being perhaps but few, this caution will have also this good in it, that it will put them upon considering and teach them the necessity of examining more than they do; without which the mind is but a receptacle of inconsistencies, not the storehouse of truths. They that do not keep up this indifference in themselves for all but truth, not supposed, but evidenced in themselves, put coloured spectacles before their eyes

[87] Here, as in section 11, the meaning is "impartiality."—F.W.G.

and look on things through false glasses, and then think themselves excused in following the false appearances which they themselves put upon them. I do not expect that by this way the assent should in everyone be proportioned to the grounds and clearness wherewith every truth is capable to be made out, or that men should be perfectly kept from error; that is more than human nature can by any means be advanced to; I aim at no such unattainable privilege; I am only speaking of what they should do who would deal fairly with their own minds and make a right use of their faculties in the pursuit of truth; we fail them a great deal more than they fail us. It is mismanagement more than want of abilities that men have reason to complain of and which they actually do complain of in those that differ from them. He that by an indifferency for all but truth suffers not his assent to go faster than his evidence, nor beyond it, will learn to examine and examine fairly instead of presuming, and nobody will be at a loss or in danger for want of embracing those truths which are necessary in his station and circumstances. In any other way but this all the world are born to orthodoxy; they imbibe at first the allowed opinions of their country and party, and so, never questioning their truth, not one of a hundred ever examines. They are applauded for presuming they are in the right. He that considers is a foe to orthodoxy, because possibly he may deviate from some of the received doctrines there. And thus men without any industry or acquisition of their own inherit local truths (for it is not the same everywhere) and are inured to assent without evidence. This influences further than is thought; for what one of a hundred of the zealous bigots in all parties ever examined the tenets he is so stiff in or ever thought it his business or duty so to do? It is suspected of lukewarmness to suppose it necessary and a tendency to apostasy to go about it. And if a man can bring his mind once to be positive and fierce for positions whose evidence he has never once examined, and that in matters of greatest concernment to him, what shall keep him from this short and easy way of being in the right in cases of less moment? Thus we are taught to clothe our minds as we do our bodies after the fashion in vogue, and it is accounted fantasticalness or something worse not to do so. This custom (which who dares oppose?) makes the short-sighted bigots and the warier sceptics,[88] as far as it prevails. And those that break from it are in danger of heresy; for, taking the whole world, how much of it does truth and orthodoxy possess together? Though it is by the last alone (which has the good luck to be everywhere) that error and heresy are judged of; for argument and evidence signify nothing in the case and excuse nowhere, but are sure to be borne down in all societies by the infallible orthodoxy of the place. Whether this be the way to truth and right assent, let the opinions that take place and prescribe in the several habitable parts of the earth declare. I never saw any reason yet why truth might not be trusted to its own evidence; I am sure, if that be not able to support it, there is no fence against error, and then truth and falsehood are but names that stand for the same things. Evidence, therefore, is that by which alone every man is (and should be) taught to regulate his assent, who is then and then only in the right way when he follows it.

Men deficient in knowledge are usually in one of these three states: either wholly ignorant; or as doubting of some proposition they have either embraced formerly

[88] That is, "makes the short-sighted [into] bigots and the warier [into] sceptics."—F.W.G.

or at present are inclined to; or, lastly, they do with assurance hold and profess without ever having examined
and being convinced by well-grounded arguments.

The first of these are in the best state of the three, by
having their minds yet in their perfect freedom and indifferency, the likelier to pursue truth the better, having
no bias yet clapped on to mislead them.[89]

35. For ignorance with an indifferency for truth is
nearer to it than opinion with ungrounded inclination,
which is the great source of error; and they are more in
danger to go out of the way who are marching under the
conduct of a guide that it is a hundred to one will mislead them, than he that has not yet taken a step and is
likelier to be prevailed on to enquire after the right way.
The last of the three sorts are in the worst condition of
all; for if a man can be persuaded and fully assured of
anything for a truth without having examined, what is
there that he may not embrace for truth? And if he has
given himself up to believe a lie, what means is there
left to recover one who can be assured without examining? To the other two this I crave leave to say that, as he
that is ignorant is in the best state of the two, so he
should pursue truth in a method suitable to that state,
i.e. by enquiring directly into the nature of the thing itself without minding the opinions of others or troubling
himself with their questions or disputes about it, but to
see what he himself can, sincerely searching after truth,
find out. He that proceeds upon others' principles in
his enquiry into any sciences, though he be resolved to
examine them and judge of them freely, does yet at least
put himself on that side and post himself in a party
which he will not quit till he be beaten out; by which

---

[89] Compare Socrates' belief that he was the wisest of men because,
though ignorant, he was aware of his ignorance.—F.W.G.

the mind is insensibly engaged to make what defence it can, and so is unawares biased. I do not say but a man should embrace some opinion when he has examined, else he examines to no purpose; but the surest and safest way is to have no opinion at all till he has examined, and that without any the least regard to the opinions or systems of other men about it. For example, were it my business to understand physic, would not the safer and readier way be to consult nature herself and inform myself in the history of diseases and their cures, than, espousing the principles of the dogmatists, methodists or chemists,[90] engage in all the disputes concerning either of those systems and suppose it true till I have tried what they can say to beat me out of it? Or supposing that Hippocrates[91] or any other book infallibly contains the whole art of physic, would not the direct way be to study, read and consider that book, weigh and compare the parts of it to find the truth, rather than espouse the doctrines of any party, who, though they acknowledge his authority, have already interpreted and wiredrawn all his text to their own sense—the tincture whereof when I have imbibed, I am more in danger to misunderstand his true meaning than if I had come to him with a mind unprepossessed by doctors and com-

90 These were different sects of physicians, whose theories derived from Graeco-Roman medicine. Dogmatists (or rationalists) based their work on rational deduction from a priori principles rather than from observation and experiment. Methodists, apparently so called because they adopted a new method which was different from either the dogmatic or the empirical, believed that health was a balance between tension and relaxation. "Chemists" used drugs or chemicals to effect their cures; Locke is probably referring more particularly to the followers of Paracelsus (see footnote 49). It should be noted that Locke himself practised as a physician.—F.W.G.

91 The great fifth century B.C. Greek physician from the island of Cos, off the coast of Asia Minor.—F.W.G.

mentators of my sect, whose reasonings, interpretation and language, which I have been used to, will of course make all chime that way and make another, and perhaps the genuine, meaning of the author seem harsh, strained and uncouth to me. For words, having naturally none of their own, carry that signification to the hearer that he is used to put upon them, whatever be the sense of him that uses them. This, I think, is visibly so; and if it be, he that begins to have any doubt of any of his tenets, which he received without examination, ought as much he can to put himself wholly into this state of ignorance in reference to that question and, throwing wholly by all his former notions and the opinions of others, examine with a perfect indifferency the question in its source without any inclination to either side or any regard to his or others' unexamined opinions. This I own is no easy thing to do; but I am not enquiring the easy way to opinion, but the right way to truth, which they must follow who will deal fairly with their own understandings and their own souls.

36. *Question.* The indifferency that I here propose will also enable them to state the question right which they are in doubt about, without which they can never come to a fair and clear decision of it.

37. *Perseverance.* Another fruit from this indifferency and the considering things in themselves abstract from our own opinions and other men's notions and discourses on them will be that each man will pursue his thoughts in that method which will be most agreeable to the nature of the thing and to his apprehension of what it suggests to him; in which he ought to proceed with regularity and constancy until he come to a well-grounded resolution wherein he may acquiesce. If it be objected that this will require every man to be a scholar

and quit all his other business and betake himself wholly to study, I answer, I propose no more to anyone than he has time for. Some men's state and condition requires no great extent of knowledge; the necessary provision for life swallows the greatest part of their time. But one man's want of leisure is no excuse for the oscitancy[92] and ignorance of those who have time to spare; and everyone has enough to get as much knowledge as is required and expected of him, and he that does not that is in love with ignorance and is accountable for it.

38. *Presumption.* The variety of distempers in men's minds is as great as of those in their bodies; some are epidemic, few escape them, and everyone too, if he would look into himself, would find some defect of his particular genius. There is scarce anyone without some idiosyncrasy that he suffers by. This man presumes upon his parts that they will not fail him at time of need, and so thinks it superfluous labour to make any provision beforehand. His understanding is to him like Fortunatus's purse,[93] which is always to furnish him without ever putting anything into it beforehand; and so he sits still satisfied without endeavouring to store his understanding with knowledge. It is the spontaneous product of the country, and what need of labour in tillage? Such men may spread their native riches before the ignorant; but they were best not come to stress and trial with the skilful. We are born ignorant of everything. The superficies of things that surround them make impressions on the negligent, but nobody penetrates into the inside without labour, attention and industry. Stones and timber

92 Literally, "yawning"; here, "laziness."—F.W.G.
93 Fortunatus was a hero of the chapbooks (popular storybooks) of the sixteenth and seventeenth centuries; he was presented by Fortune with a purse which was constantly replenished.—F.W.G.

grow of themselves, but yet there is no uniform pile with symmetry and convenience to lodge in without toil and pains. God has made the intellectual world harmonious and beautiful without us; but it will never come into our heads all at once; we must bring it home piecemeal and there set it up by our own industry, or else we shall have nothing but darkness and a chaos within, whatever order and light there be in things without us.

39. *Despondency*. On the other side there are others that depress their own minds, despond at the first difficulty, and conclude that the getting an insight in any of the sciences or making any progress in knowledge further than serves their ordinary business is above their capacities. These sit still, because they think they have not legs to go, as the others I last mentioned do, because they think they have wings to fly and can soar on high when they please. To these latter one may for answer apply the proverb, "Use legs and have legs." Nobody knows what strength of parts he has till he has tried them. And of the understanding one may most truly say that its force is greater generally than it thinks till it is put to it. *Viresque acquirit eundo*.[94]

And therefore the proper remedy here is but to set the mind to work and apply the thoughts vigorously to the business; for it holds in the struggles of the mind as in those of war, *dum putant se vincere vicere*.[95] A persuasion that we shall overcome any difficulties that we meet with in the sciences seldom fails to carry us through them. Nobody knows the strength of his mind and the force of steady and regular application till he has tried.

[94] "It increases in strength as it goes" (Vergil, *Aeneid*, IV, 175; from a description of rumour).—F.W.G.

[95] "So long as they thought they were winning, they did win" (Livy, II, 64).—F.W.G.

This is certain, he that sets out upon weak legs will not only go further but grow stronger too than one who, with a vigorous constitution and firm limbs, only sits still.

Something of kin to this men may observe in themselves when the mind frights itself (as it often does) with anything reflected on in gross and transiently viewed confusedly and at a distance. Things thus offered to the mind carry the show of nothing but difficulty in them and are thought to be wrapped up in impenetrable obscurity. But the truth is, these are nothing but spectres that the understanding raises to itself to flatter its own laziness. It sees nothing distinctly in things remote and in a huddle, and therefore concludes too faintly that there is nothing more clear to be discovered in them. It is but to approach nearer, and that mist of our own raising that enveloped them will remove; and those that in that mist appeared hideous giants not to be grappled with will be found to be of the ordinary and natural size and shape. Things that in a remote and confused view seem very obscure must be approached by gentle and regular steps, and what is most visible, easy and obvious in them first considered. Reduce them into their distinct parts, and then in their due order bring all that should be known concerning every one of those parts into plain and simple questions; and then what was thought obscure, perplexed and too hard for our weak parts will lay itself open to the understanding in a fair view and let the mind into that which before it was awed with and kept at a distance from as wholly mysterious. I appeal to my reader's experience whether this has never happened to him, especially when, busy on one thing, he has occasionally reflected on another. I ask him whether he has never thus been scared with a sudden opinion of mighty difficulties, which yet have vanished when he has seriously and methodically applied himself to the consideration of this seeming terrible subject; and there has been no other matter of astonishment left, but that he amused himself with so discouraging a prospect of his own raising about a matter which in the handling was found to have nothing in it more strange nor intricate than several other things which he had long since and with ease mastered. This experience should teach us how to deal with such bugbears another time, which should rather serve to excite our vigour than enervate our industry. The surest way for a learner in this as in all other cases is not to advance by jumps and large strides; let that which he sets himself to learn next be indeed the next, i.e. as nearly conjoined with what he knows already as is possible; let it be distinct but not remote from it; let it be new and what he did not know before, that the understanding may advance; but let it be as little at once as may be, that its advances may be clear and sure. All the ground that it gets this way it will hold. This distinct gradual growth in knowledge is firm and sure; it carries its own light with it in every step of its progression in any easy and orderly train, than which there is nothing of more use to the understanding. And though this perhaps may seem a very slow and lingering way to knowledge, yet I dare confidently affirm that whoever will try it in himself or anyone he will teach shall find the advances greater in this method than they would in the same space of time have been in any other he could have taken. The greatest part of true knowledge lies in a distinct perception of things in themselves distinct. And some men give more clear light and knowledge by the bare distinct stating of a question than others by talking of it in gross whole hours together. In this, they who so state a question do no more but separate and disentangle the parts of it one from another and lay them, when so disentangled, in their due order. This often, without any more ado, resolves the doubt and shews the mind where the truth lies. The agreement or disagreement of the ideas in question, when they are once separated and distinctly considered, is in many cases presently perceived and thereby clear and lasting knowledge gained;[96] whereas things in gross taken up together, and so lying together in confusion, can produce in the mind but a confused, which is in effect no, knowledge; or at least, when it comes to be examined and made use of, will prove little better than none. I therefore take the liberty to repeat here again what I have said elsewhere,[97] that in learning anything as little should be proposed to the mind at once as is possible; and, that being understood and fully mastered, to proceed to the next adjoining part yet unknown, [a] simple, unperplexed proposition belonging to the matter in hand and tending to the clearing what is principally designed.[98]

40. *Analogy.*[99] Anology is of great use to the mind in

[96] See footnote 38.—F.W.G.

[97] For example, in section 28 and in *Thoughts,* §§ 64–66, 167 ff.

[98] The text in the latter part of this sentence is obscure; the simplest emendation is to add "a" before "simple," but this still leaves some difficulty. Fowler, *op. cit.,* and Adamson, *op. cit.,* print the text as it stands; the former suggests that from "simple, unperplexed proposition" to the end of the sentence is either in apposition to "part yet unknown" or an independent absolute participial expression; the latter suggests the following emendation: "and, that being understood and fully mastered, to proceed to the next adjoining part yet unknown; [to state] what is belonging to the matter in hand as simple, unperplexed proposition [s, and so] tending to clear it, [is] what is principally designed."—F.W.G.

[99] Argument by analogy involves inference from resemblance or similarity: A and B are alike in respect of x and y; A possesses a

many cases, especially in natural philosophy, and that part of it chiefly which consists in happy and successful experiments. But here we must take care that we keep ourselves within that wherein the analogy consists. For example, the acid oil of vitriol is found to be good in such a case, therefore the spirit of nitre or vinegar may be used in the like case. If the good effect of it be owing wholly to the acidity of it, the trial may be justified; but if there be something else besides the acidity in the oil of vitriol, which produces the good we desire in the case, we mistake that for analogy which is not and suffer our understanding to be misguided by a wrong supposition of analogy where there is none.

41. *Association.* Though I have, in the second book[100] of my *Essay Concerning Human Understanding,* treated of the association of ideas, yet having done it there historically,[101] as giving a view of the understanding in this as well as its several other ways of operating, rather than designing there to enquire into the remedies [that] ought to be applied to it, it will, under this latter consideration, afford other matter of thought to those who have a mind to instruct themselves thoroughly in the right way of conducting their understandings; and that the rather because this, if I mistake not, is as frequent a cause of mistake and error in us as perhaps anything else that can be named, and is a disease of the mind as hard to be cured as any, it being a very hard thing to

---

quality z, therefore B also has it. It is sometimes useful, but often dangerous. The argument in Locke's illustration runs thus: sulphuric acid is found to have a certain effect; nitric and acetic acids, being also acids, may be assumed to have the same effect. But, as Locke says, the argument is valid only if the effect is due wholly to the acidity.—F.W.G.

100 Chapter xxxiii.—F.W.G.

101 That is, as a systematic statement of fact.—F.W.G.

convince anyone that things are not so, and naturally so, as they constantly appear to him.

By this one easy and unheeded miscarriage of the understanding sandy and loose foundations become infallible principles and will not suffer themselves to be touched or questioned; such unnatural connections become by custom as natural to the mind as sun and light. Fire and warmth go together and so seem to carry with them as natural an evidence as self-evident truths themselves.[102] And where then shall one with hopes of success begin the cure? Many men firmly embrace falsehood for truth, not only because they never thought otherwise, but also because, thus blinded as they have been from the beginning, they never could think otherwise, at least without a vigour of mind able to contest the empire of habit and look into its own principles—a freedom which few men have the notion of in themselves and fewer are allowed the practice of by others, it being the great art and business of the teachers and guides in most sects to suppress as much as they can this fundamental duty which every man owes himself and is the first steady step towards right and truth in the whole train of his actions and opinions. This would give one reason to suspect that such teachers are conscious to themselves of the falsehood or weakness of the tenets they profess, since they will not suffer the grounds whereon they are built to be examined; whereas those who seek truth only and desire to own and propagate nothing else freely expose their principles to the test, are pleased to have them examined, give men leave to

---

102 Adamson, *op. cit.*, has: ". . . questioned; such unnatural connections become by custom as natural to the mind as [that] sun and light, fire and warmth go together, and so seem to carry with them. . . ."—F.W.G.

reject them if they can; and if there be anything weak
and unsound in them, are willing to have it detected,
that they themselves, as well as others, may not lay any
stress upon any received proposition beyond what the
evidence of its truth will warrant and allow.

There is, I know, a great fault among all sorts of people of principling their children and scholars, which at
last, when looked into, amounts to no more but making
them imbibe their teacher's notions and tenets by an
implicit faith and firmly to adhere to them whether true
or false. What colours may be given to this or of what
use it may be when practised upon the vulgar, destined
to labour and given up to the service of their bellies, I
will not here enquire. But as to the ingenuous[103] part of
mankind, whose condition allows them leisure and letters
and enquiry after truth, I can see no other right way of
principling them but to take heed as much as may be
that in their tender years ideas that have no natural co-
hesion come not to be united in their heads; and that
this rule be often inculcated to them to be their guide in
the whole course of their lives and studies, viz., that they
never suffer any ideas to be joined in their understandings in any other or stronger combination than what
their own nature[104] and correspondence give them, and
that they often examine those that they find linked together in their minds, whether this association of ideas
be from the visible agreement that is in the ideas themselves or from the habitual and prevailing custom of the
mind joining them thus together in thinking.

This is for caution against this evil, before it be thor-

---

[103] Locke uses this word in a number of distinguishable senses in
his writings; here it seems to mean "of honourable birth," "upper
class."—F.W.G.
[104] That is, the nature of the ideas.—F.W.G.

oughly riveted by custom in the understanding; but he that would cure it when habit has established it must nicely[105] observe the very quick and almost imperceptible motions of the mind in its habitual actions. What I have said in another place[106] about the change of the ideas of sense into those of judgement may be proof of this. Let anyone not skilled in painting be told, when he sees bottles and tobacco pipes and other things so painted as they are in some places shown, that he does not see protuberances, and you will not convince him but by the touch; he will not believe that by an instantaneous legerdemain of his own thoughts one idea is substituted for the other. How frequent instances may one meet with of this in the arguings of the learned, who not seldom, in two ideas that they have been accustomed to join in their minds, substitute one for the other; and, I am apt to think, often without perceiving it themselves. This, whilst they are under the deceit of it, makes them incapable of conviction, and they applaud themselves as zealous champions for truth when indeed they are contending for error. And the confusion of two different ideas, which a customary connection of them in their minds has made to them almost one, fills their head with false views and their reasonings with false consequences.

42. *Fallacies.* Right understanding consists in the discovery and adherence to truth, and that in the perception of the visible or probable agreement or disagreement of ideas as they are affirmed and denied one of another.[107] From whence it is evident that the right use and conduct of the understanding, whose business is purely truth and nothing else, is that the mind should be

105 That is, "precisely."—F.W.G.
106 *Essay*, II, ix.
107 See footnote 38.—F.W.G.

kept in a perfect indifferency, not inclining to either side
any further than evidence settles it by knowledge or the
over-balance of probability gives it the turn of assent
and belief; but yet it is very hard to meet with any discourse wherein one may not perceive the author not
only maintain (for that is reasonable and fit), but inclined and biased to one side of the question with marks
of a desire that that should be true. If it be asked me
how authors who have such a bias and lean to it may be
discovered, I answer, by observing how in their writings
or arguings they are often led by their inclinations to
change the ideas of the question, either by changing the
terms or by adding and joining others to them, whereby
the ideas under consideration are so varied as to be more
serviceable to their purpose and to be thereby brought
to an easier and nearer agreement or more visible and re-
moter disagreement one with another. This is plain and
direct sophistry; but I am far from thinking that, wherever it is found, it is made use of with design to deceive
and mislead the readers. It is visible that men's prejudices and inclinations by this way impose often upon
themselves; and their affection for truth, under their
prepossession in favour of one side, is the very thing
that leads them from it. Inclination suggests and slides
into their discourse favourable terms which introduce
favourable ideas, till at last by this means that is concluded clear and evident, thus dressed up, which taken
in its native state, by making use of none but the precise
determined ideas, would find no admittance at all. The
putting these glosses on what they affirm, these (as they
are thought) handsome, easy and graceful explications
of what they are discoursing on, is so much the character
of what is called and esteemed writing well, that it is
very hard to think that authors will ever be persuaded to

leave what serves so well to propagate their opinions and procure themselves credit in the world for a more jejune and dry way of writing, by keeping to the same terms precisely annexed to the same ideas, a sour and blunt stiffness tolerable in mathematicians only, who force their way and make truth prevail by irresistible demonstration.

But yet, if authors cannot be prevailed with to quit the looser, though more insinuating, ways of writing, if they will not think fit to keep close to truth and instruction by unvaried terms and plain unsophisticated arguments, yet it concerns readers not to be imposed on by fallacies and the prevailing ways of insinuation. To do this, the surest and most effectual remedy is to fix in the mind the clear and distinct ideas of the question stripped of words; and so likewise in the train of argumentation, to take up the author's ideas, neglecting his words, observing how they connect or separate those in the question. He that does this will be able to cast off all that is superfluous; he will see what is pertinent, what coherent, what is direct to, what slides by the question. This will readily show him all the foreign ideas in the discourse and where they were brought in; and though they perhaps dazzled the writer, yet he will perceive that they give no light nor strength to his reasonings.

This, though it be the shortest and easiest way of reading books with profit and keeping oneself from being misled by great names or plausible discourses, yet, it being hard and tedious to those who have not accustomed themselves to it, it is not to be expected that everyone (amongst those few who really pursue truth) should this way guard his understanding from being imposed on by the wilful or at least undesigned sophistry which creeps into most of the books of argument. They that write against their conviction or that, next to them, are resolved to maintain the tenets of a party they are engaged in cannot be supposed to reject any arms that may help to defend their cause, and therefore such should be read with the greatest caution. And they who write for opinions they are sincerely persuaded of and believe to be true think they may so far allow themselves to indulge their laudable affection to truth as to permit their esteem of it to give it the best colours and set it off with the best expressions and dress they can, thereby to gain it the easiest entrance into the minds of their readers and fix it deepest there.

One of those being the state of mind we may justly suppose most writers to be in, it is fit their readers, who apply to them for instruction, should not lay by that caution which becomes[108] a sincere pursuit of truth, and should make them always watchful against whatever might conceal or misrepresent it. If they have not the skill of representing to themselves the author's sense by pure ideas separated from sounds and thereby divested of the false lights[109] and deceitful ornaments of speech, this yet they should do: they should keep the precise question steadily in their minds, carry it along with them through the whole discourse, and suffer not the least alteration in the terms either by addition, subtraction or substituting any other. This everyone can do who has a mind to it; and he that has not a mind to it, it is plain makes his understanding only the warehouse of other men's lumber—I mean false and unconcluding reasonings, rather than a repository of truth for his own

---

[108] That is, "befits."

[109] Adamson, *op. cit.*, suggests that the image here is that of wreckers' beacons, which were lit to lure vessels on to the rocks.— F.W.G.

use, which will prove substantial and stand him in stead when he has occasion for it. And whether such a one deals fairly by his own mind and conducts his own understanding right, I leave to his own understanding to judge.

43. *Fundamental verities.* The mind of men being very narrow and so slow in making acquaintance with things and taking in new truths that no one man is capable, in a much longer life than ours, to know all truths, it becomes our prudence in our search after knowledge to employ our thoughts about fundamental and material questions, carefully avoiding those that are trifling and not suffering ourselves to be diverted from our main even purpose by those that are merely incidental. How much of many young men's time is thrown away in purely logical enquiries, I need not mention.[110] This is no better than if a man who was to be a painter should spend all his time in examining the threads of the several cloths he is to paint upon and counting the hairs of each pencil and brush he intends to use in the laying on of his colours. Nay, it is much worse than for a young painter to spend his apprenticeship in such useless niceties; for he, at the end of all his pains to no purpose, finds that it is not painting nor any help to it, and so is really to no purpose. Whereas men designed for scholars have often their heads so filled and warmed with disputes on logical questions, that they take those airy useless notions for real and substantial knowledge and think their understandings so well furnished with science that they need not look any further into the nature of things or descend to the mechanical drudgery of

110 Locke has his own education in mind. He frequently deprecates the logical exercises which were a regular part of university studies. See footnote 32 and *Thoughts*, §§ 94, 98, 188–189.—F.W.G.

experiment and enquiry. This is so obvious a mismanagement of the understanding, and that in the professed way to knowledge, that it could not be passed by; to which might be joined abundance of questions and the way of handling of them in the schools. What faults in particular of this kind every man is or may be guilty of would be infinite to enumerate; it suffices to have shown that superficial and slight discoveries and observations that contain nothing of moment in themselves, nor serve as clues to lead us into further knowledge, should be lightly passed by and never thought worth our searching after.

There are fundamental truths that lie at the bottom, the basis upon which a great many others rest and in which they have their consistency. These are teeming truths, rich in store with which they furnish the mind, and, like the lights of heaven, are not only beautiful and entertaining in themselves, but give light and evidence to other things that without them could not be seen or known. Such is that admirable discovery of Mr. Newton,[111] that all bodies gravitate to one another, which may be counted as the basis of natural philosophy; which of what use it is to the understanding of the great frame of our solar system he has to the astonishment of the learned world shown; and how much further it would guide us in other things, if rightly pursued, is not yet known. Our Saviour's great rule, that we should love our neighbour as ourselves, is such a fundamental truth for the regulating human society, that, I think, by that alone one might without difficulty de-

[111] Locke was a friend of Newton and had a great respect for him. In *Thoughts,* (§ 194) he writes of "the incomparable Mr. Newton," and in the *Essay* he describes the *Principia* (published in 1687) as "his never enough to be admired book."—F.W.G.

termine all the cases and doubts in social morality. These and such as these are the truths we should endeavour to find out and store our minds with. Which leads me to another thing in the conduct of the understanding that is no less necessary, viz.:

44. *Bottoming.* To accustom ourselves in any question proposed to examine and find out upon what it bottoms. Most of the difficulties that come in our way, when well considered and traced, lead us to some proposition which, known to be true, clears the doubt and gives an easy solution of the question; whilst topical[112] and superficial arguments, of which there is store to be found on both sides, filling the head with variety of thoughts and the mouth with copious discourse serve only to amuse the understanding and entertain company without coming to the bottom of the question, the only place of rest and stability for an inquisitive mind whose tendency is only to truth and knowledge.

For example, if it be demanded whether the Grand Seignior[113] can lawfully take what he will from any of his people, this question cannot be resolved without coming to a certainty whether all men are naturally equal; for upon that it turns, and that truth, well settled in the understanding and carried in the mind through the various debates concerning the various rights of men in society, will go a great way in putting an end to them and showing on which side the truth is.

45. *Transferring of thoughts.* There is scarce anything more for the improvement of knowledge, for the ease of life and the dispatch of business than for a man

112 See footnote 32.—F.W.G.

113 The Turkish Sultan; but no doubt Locke is thinking of the English monarchy. He discusses the question in his *Two Treatises of Government.*—F.W.G.

to be able to dispose of his own thoughts; and there is scarce anything harder in the whole conduct of the understanding than to get a full mastery over it. The mind in a waking man has always some object that it applies itself to, which, when we are lazy or unconcerned, we can easily change and at pleasure transfer our thoughts to another, and from thence to a third which has no relation to either of the former. Hence men forwardly conclude and frequently say, nothing is so free as thought; and it were well it were so; but the contrary will be found true in several instances; and there are many cases wherein there is nothing more resty[114] and ungovernable than our thoughts; they will not be directed what objects to pursue nor be taken off from those they have once fixed on, but run away with a man in pursuit of those ideas they have in view, let him do what he can.

I will not here mention again what I have above taken notice of,[115] how hard it is to get the mind, narrowed by a custom of thirty or forty years standing to a scanty collection of obvious and common ideas, to enlarge itself to a more copious stock and grow into an acquaintance with those that would afford more abundant matter of useful contemplation; it is not of this I am here speaking. The inconvenience I would here represent and find a remedy for is the difficulty there is sometimes to transfer our minds from one subject to another in cases where the ideas are equally familiar to us.

Matters that are recommended to our thoughts by any of our passions take possession of our minds with a kind of authority and will not be kept out or dislodged, but, as if the passion that rules were for the time the

114 That is, "restive," "intractable."—F.W.G.
115 Section 3.—F.W.G.

sheriff of the place and came with all the posse,[116] the understanding is seized and taken with the object it introduces, as if it had a legal right to be alone considered there. There is scarce anybody, I think, of so calm a temper who has not some time found this tyranny on his understanding and suffered under the inconvenience of it. Who is there almost whose mind at some time or another love or anger, fear or grief has not so fastened to some clog, that it could not turn itself to any other object? I call it a clog, for it hangs upon the mind so as to hinder its vigour and activity in the pursuit of other contemplations, and advances itself little or not [at] all in the knowledge of the thing which it so closely hugs and constantly pores on. Men thus possessed are sometimes as if they were so in the worst sense and lay under the power of an enchantment. They see not what passes before their eyes, hear not the audible discourse of the company; and when by any strong application to them they are roused a little, they are like men brought to themselves from some remote region; whereas in truth they come no further than their secret cabinet within, where they have been wholly taken up with the puppet which is for that time appointed for their entertainment. The shame that such dumps cause to well bred people, when it carries them away from the company where they should bear a part in the conversation, is a sufficient argument that it is a fault in the conduct of our understanding not to have that power over it as to make use of it to those purposes and on those occasions wherein we have need of its assistance. The mind should be always free and ready to turn

116 The *posse comitatus* was a force of men whom the sheriff of the county (*comitatus*) could call on to assist him in keeping order. —F.W.G.

itself to the variety of objects that occur and allow them as much consideration as shall for that time be thought fit. To be engrossed so by one object as not to be prevailed on to leave it for another that we judge fitter for our contemplation is to make it of no use to us. Did this state of mind remain always so, everyone would without scruple give it the name of perfect madness; and while it does last, at whatever intervals it returns, such a rotation of thoughts about the same object no more carries us forwards towards the attainment of knowledge than getting upon a mill horse whilst he jogs on in his circular tract would carry a man on a journey.

I grant something must be allowed to legitimate passions and to natural inclinations. Every man, besides occasional affections, has beloved studies, and those the mind will more closely stick to; but yet it is best that it should be always at liberty and under the free disposal of the man to act how and upon what he directs. This we should endeavour to obtain, unless we would be content with such a flaw in our understandings that sometimes we should be as it were without it;[117] for it is very little better than so in cases where we cannot make use of it to those purposes we would and which stand in present need of it.

But before fit remedies can be thought on for this disease, we must know the several causes of it and thereby regulate the cure, if we will hope to labour with success.

One we have already instanced in, whereof all men that reflect have so general a knowledge and so often an experience in themselves, that nobody doubts of it. A prevailing passion so pins down our thoughts to the object and concern of it, that a man passionately in

117 That is, without our understanding.—F.W.G.

love cannot bring himself to think of his ordinary affairs, nor a kind mother drooping under the loss of a child is not able to bear a part as she was wont in the discourse of the company or conversation of her friends.

But though passion be the most obvious and general, yet it is not the only cause that binds up the understanding and confines it for the time to one object, from which it will not be taken off.

Besides this, we may often find that the understanding, when it has a while employed itself upon a subject which either chance or some slight accident offered to it without the interest or recommendation of any passion, works itself into a warmth and by degrees gets into a career, wherein, like a bowl down a hill, it increases its motion by going and will not be stopped or diverted, though, when the heat is over, it sees all this earnest application was about a trifle not worth a thought and all the pains employed about it lost labour.

There is a third sort, if I mistake not, yet lower than this; it is a sort of childishness, if I may so say, of the understanding, wherein, during the fit, it plays with and dandles some insignificant puppet to no end nor with any design at all, and yet cannot easily be got off from it. Thus some trivial sentence or a scrap of poetry will sometimes get into men's heads and make such a chiming there, that there is no stilling of it, no peace to be obtained nor attention to anything else, but this impertinent[118] guest will take up the mind and possess the thoughts in spite of all endeavours to get rid of it. Whether everyone has experimented[119] in themselves this troublesome intrusion of some striking ideas which thus importune the understanding and hinder it from

118 That is, "irrelevant," "not pertinent."—F.W.G.
119 That is, "experienced."—F.W.G.

being better employed, I know not. But persons of
very good parts, and those more than one, I have heard
speak and complain of it themselves. The reason I
have to make this doubt is from what I have known in
a case something of kin to this, though much odder,
and that is of a sort of visions that some people have
lying quiet but perfectly awake in the dark or with their
eyes shut. It is a great variety of faces, most commonly
very odd ones, that appear to them in train one after
another, so that, having had just the sight of one, it immediately passes away to give place to another that
the same instant succeeds and has as quick an exit as its
leader; and so they march on in a constant succession;
nor can any one of them by any endeavour be stopped or
retained beyond the instant of its appearance, but is
thrust out by its follower, which will have its turn. Concerning this fantastical phenomenon I have talked with
several people, whereof some have been perfectly acquainted with it and others have been so wholly
strangers to it, that they could hardly be brought to conceive or believe it. I knew a lady of excellent parts
who had got past thirty without having ever had the
least notice of any such thing. She was so great a stranger
to it that, when she heard me and another talking of
it, could scarce forbear thinking we bantered her; but
some time after, drinking a large dose of dilute tea (as
she was ordered by a physician) going to bed, she told
us at next meeting that she had now experimented
what our discourse had much ado to persuade her of. She
had seen a great variety of faces in a long train succeed-
ing one another, as we had described; they were all
strangers and intruders, such as she had no acquaintance
with before nor sought after then, and as they came of
themselves they went too; none of them stayed a mo-

ment nor could be detained by all the endeavours she could use, but went on in their solemn procession, just appeared and then vanished. This odd phenomenon seems to have a mechanical cause, and to depend upon the matter and motion of the blood or animal spirits.[120]

When the fancy is bound by passion, I know no way to set the mind free and at liberty to prosecute what thoughts the man would make choice of, but to allay the present passion or counterbalance it with another, which is an art to be got by study and acquaintance with the passions.

Those who find themselves apt to be carried away with the spontaneous current of their own thoughts, not excited by any passion or interest, must be very wary and careful in all the instances of it to stop it and never humour their minds in being thus triflingly busy. Men know the value of their corporal liberty and therefore suffer not willingly fetters and chains to be put upon them. To have the mind captivated is, for the time, certainly the greater evil of the two and deserves our utmost care and endeavours to preserve the freedom of our better part. And in this case our pains will not be lost; striving and struggling will prevail, if we constantly in all such occasions make use of it. We must never indulge these trivial attentions of thought; as soon as we find the mind makes itself a business of nothing, we should immediately disturb and check it, introduce new and more serious considerations, and not leave till we have beaten it off from the pursuit it was upon. This at first, if we have let the contrary practice grow to a

[120] According to some ancient physicians an extremely rarefied substance, which they called "animal spirits," was produced by the brain and flowed along the nerves to effect the operations of senses and muscles; it also effected the operation of the soul or higher intellectual functions.—F.W.G.

habit, will perhaps be difficult; but constant endeavours will by degrees prevail and at last make it easy. And when a man is pretty well advanced and can command his mind off at pleasure from incidental and undesigned pursuits, it may not be amiss for him to go on further and make attempts upon meditations of greater moment, that at the last he may have a full power over his own mind, and be so fully master of his own thoughts as to be able to transfer them from one subject to another with the same ease that he can lay by anything he has in his hand and take something else that he has a mind to in the room of it. This liberty of mind is of great use both in business and study, and he that has got it will have no small advantage of ease and dispatch in all that is the chosen and useful employment of his understanding.

The third and last way which I mentioned the mind to be sometimes taken up with (I mean the chiming of some particular words or sentence in the memory and, as it were, making a noise in the head, and the like) seldom happens but when the mind is lazy or very loosely and negligently employed. It were better indeed be without such impertinent and useless repetitions; any obvious idea, when it is roving causelessly at a venture, being of more use and apter to suggest something worth consideration than the insignificant buzz of purely empty sounds. But since the rousing of the mind and setting the understanding on work with some degrees of vigour does for the most part presently set it free from these idle companions, it may not be amiss, whenever we find ourselves troubled with them, to make use of so profitable a remedy that is always at hand.

Index

FRANCIS W. GARFORTH, Lecturer in Education at the University of Hull, England, was born in Ceylon in 1917. He received his B.A. from the University of London and his M.A. from Cambridge University. After teaching in secondary schools for ten years, he joined the university's Department of Education in 1949. Mr. Garforth is the author of *Education and Social Purpose* (1962), and he edited the volumes *Locke's Thoughts Concerning Education* (1964) and *John Dewey: Selected Educational Writings* (1966).